BASICS
INTERIOR ARCHITECTURE

Form and Structure in Interior Architecture

Second Edition

Fairchild Books
An imprint of Bloomsbury Publishing PLC

B L O O M S B U R Y
LONDON · OXFORD · NEW YORK · NEW DELHI · SYDNEY

Fairchild Books
An imprint of Bloomsbury Publishing Plc

Imprint previously known as AVA Publishing

50 Bedford Square	1385 Broadway
London	New York
WC1B 3DP	NY 10018
UK	USA

www.bloomsbury.com

**FAIRCHILD BOOKS, BLOOMSBURY and the Diana
logo are trademarks of Bloomsbury Publishing Plc**

First published by AVA Publishing SA, 2007
This 2nd edition is published by Fairchild Books,
an imprint of Bloomsbury Publishing Plc

© Bloomsbury Publishing Plc, 2016

Graeme Brooker and Sally Stone have asserted their right
under the Copyright, Designs and Patents Act, 1988, to be
identified as Authors of this work.

British Library Cataloguing-in-Publication Data
A catalogue record for this book is available from the
British Library.

ISBN:	PB:	978-1-472572-65-3
	ePDF:	978-1-472572-66-0

Library of Congress Cataloging-in-Publication Data
Brooker, Graeme.
Form and structure in interior architecture / Graeme
Brooker and Sally Stone. — Second edition.
pages cm
First published 2007.
ISBN 978-1-4725-7265-3 (pbk.) — ISBN 978-1-4725-
7266-0 (epdf) — 1. Interior architecture. I. Stone, Sally.
II. Title.
NA2850.B75 2015
729—dc23
2015011345

Series: Basics Interior Architecture

Layout by Saxon Graphics Ltd, Derby
Printed and bound in China

0.1
_____

Name: D.E. Shaw Office and
Trading Area, reception
Location: New York, USA
Designer: Steven Holl

0.1

Contents

Introduction

The aim of this book is to provide a focused, informative, and readable investigation into the practice of designing interior space. Interior architecture is a subject that encompasses the analysis and understanding of existing buildings and proposed spaces, the nature and qualities of an interior space, and an intimate examination of the characteristics of interior decoration. *Form and Structure in Interior Architecture* will reveal the process of organizing and redesigning a particular space or spaces, and will break down this practice into its constituent parts, with a particular emphasis upon issues of form and structure. Each section will focus on the space, but will also deal with a particular aspect of the redesigning process. It will argue that the way forward for interior design is a method based upon process rather than function. An approach based upon a perceptive and discriminating reading of the existing or proposed space can produce both dynamic and appropriate results.

0.2

Name: ING & NNH offices
Location: Budapest, Hungary
Designer: Erick van Egeraat (EEA)

0.2

1.1

1 The Design Process

Unlike many other design- and art-based disciplines, which often begin with the theoretical stance of the artist, the design of an interior is always influenced by the experience of the place that it is to inhabit. The practice of designing interiors is an intricate process of satisfying the needs of the users, while balancing this with considerations of situation and place. This opening chapter will introduce the notion of interior architecture, interior design, and the strategic reuse of buildings. It will examine the fundamental ideas that underpin the design of interior space, and will also clarify the different approaches to conservation: from the preservation of the building in its found condition to the comprehensive redevelopment of the whole structure.

1.1

Name: Groeninge Museum
Location: Bruges, Belgium
Designer: 514NE

Introduction

Definitions and descriptions

Interior architecture, interior design, and building reuse are all disciplines that deal with the development and design of interior space. The interior architect or designer will transform a given space, whether the crumbling ruins of an ancient building or the drawn parameters of a building proposal. This complex process requires an understanding of the qualities of the given existing building, while simultaneously combining these factors with the functional requirements of new users. Before looking in more detail at how the interior architect or designer does this, it is essential that the various interpretations of the subject are carefully analyzed and understood.

Interior design is a term that has traditionally been used to describe all types of interior projects. This would have included everything from decoration to remodeling. However, in view of the fact that building reuse has become such a highly regarded practice, it has clearly become necessary to divide the main subject and define more clearly the individual specialisms: interior architecture and design. Processes that deal with the manipulation of the three-dimensional volume must not be confused with interior decoration, which generally concentrates on furniture and finishes.

1.2

1.2

Castelvecchio Museum, Verona, Italy

Reuse and redesign

The reuse of existing buildings and the redesign of spaces within them are subjects that are central to the evolution of the urban environment, and issues of conservation and sustainability have become vital to the development of cities. As the manner in which the urban environment has changed, so the prevailing attitude towards building reuse has also altered.

There are a number of different methods used in the conservation of a structure, and there are distinct differences between each approach: preservation maintains the building in the found state; restoration is the process of returning the condition of the building to its original state; renovation is the practice of renewing and updating a building, and remodeling, or adaptation, is the process of wholeheartedly altering a building. Sometimes, two of the methods may be employed in unison, for example, when designing the Sackler Galleries, Royal Academy of Arts. At these galleries, Foster Associates ensured that the façades of the original buildings were completely restored before embarking on the remodeling of the space.

It is important that the designer is aware of the requirements of the new users of the building or space. Without an understanding of these, it is not easy to establish the exact qualities of design required, and it is difficult to appreciate whether a relationship with the original building can be established.

1.3

Sackler Galleries,
Royal Academy of Arts, London, UK

1.3

Definitions and Descriptions

Interior architecture, interior design, and interior decoration are all practices that deal, in varying degrees, with an existing space or building. This section outlines the nuances between the different disciplines.

Interior architecture

Name: Tate Modern
Location: London, UK
Designer: Herzog & de Meuron

Interior architecture is concerned only with the remodeling of existing buildings; that is the development of attitudes towards existing spaces and structures, building reuse, and organizational principles. It bridges the practices of interior design and architecture, often dealing with complex structural, environmental, and servicing problems. This practice encompasses a huge range of project types, from museums, galleries, and other public buildings, through office and other commercial buildings to domestic developments.

When remodeling the enormous Bankside Power Station for use as an art gallery, the approach Herzog & de Meuron took was to accentuate the particularly huge and industrial qualities of the building. The gallery spaces occupy the appropriate rooms around the edge of the building, while the vast turbine hall has become an internal public street. The most dramatic and obvious element of the remodeling is the insertion of a massive lantern, or glazed roof, which hovers along the central axis of the building. It functions as a lightwell during the day, throwing natural light into the public space at the center of the gallery, and at night it appears to glow with the latent energy of the obsolete power station. Although the function of the building has completely changed, the inherent qualities of it have not: the same massive, strong, and powerful characteristics of the power station have been transferred to the gallery.

1.4a

1.4b

1.4a

In the interior of the Tate Modern, the new lightweight glazed lantern hovers above the sheer bulk of the existing building.

1.4b

Natural light flows through the axial lantern of the turbine hall.

1.4c

The massive public space in the turbine hall is apparent in this cutaway drawing.

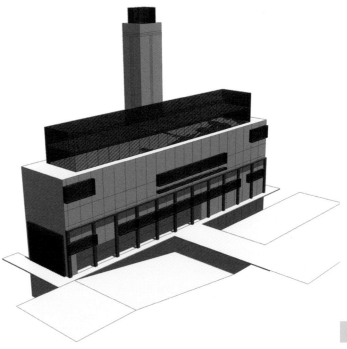

1.4c

1.5a

Interior design

Name: Children's Galleries, Science Museum
Location: London, UK
Designer: Ben Kelly Design

Interior design is an interdisciplinary practice concerned with the creation of a range of interior environments that articulate identity and atmosphere through the manipulation of spatial volume, placement of specific elements, such as furniture, and the treatment of surfaces. It generally describes projects that require little or no structural changes to the existing building, although there are many exceptions to this. The original space is very much retained in its original structural state and the new interior is inserted within it. It often has an ephemeral quality and typically would encompass such projects as retail, exhibition, domestic, and office interiors.

In their design of the Children's Galleries at the Science Museum, Ben Kelly Design has developed a distinct approach to interior design that is based upon the manipulation and reuse of found objects, combined with an explicit sense of structure and a desire to expose the truth about a particular situation or space. The practice became known for the "industrial chic" look that was developed in the 1980s for the infamous Haçienda club and Dry 201 bar in Manchester, UK. The Children's Galleries at the Science Museum adopt that same attitude: the space has been stripped down to leave only the essential elements; that is, the raw walls, floors, and ceiling. The ducts, cables, and other services are revealed—even the cladding around the lift has been removed so that workings are exposed. The space has then been animated with "industrial" objects and motifs to create an open place where children can feel sufficiently relaxed to enjoy themselves, yet suitably stimulated to become curious.

"Interior design had come to the forefront of public design-consciousness through its leadership of the retail revolution."

Anne Massey

1.5b

1.5c

1.5a

The basement terrace is animated through occupation.

1.5b

Three-dimensional drawing showing the formal collection of carefully placed objects.

1.5c

The rhythm of the existing building dictates the position of the distinct spaces within the new interior.

1.5d

Ben Kelly uses a palette of industrial materials.

1.5d

1.6a

The heavily decorated chancel contains the new brass corona, the iron sanctuary gates, and the carved stone altar.

1.6a

Interior decoration

Name: St Peter's Cathedral
Location: Lancaster, UK
Designer: Francis Roberts Architects

Interior decoration is the art of decorating interior spaces or rooms to impart a particular character that fits well with the existing architecture. Interior decoration is concerned with such issues as surface pattern, ornament, furniture, soft furnishings, lighting, and materials. It generally deals only with minor structural changes to the existing building. Typical examples of this practice are the design of domestic, hotel, and restaurant interiors.

A very fine example of professional decoration is the project for St Peter's Cathedral, Lancaster. The Victorian cathedral was reordered in the 1970s and many of its artefacts were taken away. Francis Roberts Architects completely restored the building in 1995; they redecorated it in a Gothic Revival style, and designed new furniture, and artefacts. The decoration on the walls and ceiling is appropriate to the style of architecture. The exposed beams and other

1.6b

The qualities of space and light are revealed in this drawing.

1.6b

structures are intricately painted and gilded; the ceiling and walls are more simply decorated with stenciled motifs. The new furniture includes a carved stone altar, brass corona, and iron sanctuary gates.

This project was completed in September 1995 and received a RIBA award in 1996. A review of the project was published in *Church Building*, January 1996: "…here is an architect who understands the fin de siècle architectural mind not only in an extremely thorough, but also practical way. He can actually create buildings in that design-language; the rest of us can only talk about it."

Reuse and Redesign

This section on reuse and redesign discusses the various approaches to the creation of interior space within buildings. It outlines practices from preservation, right the way through to the creative adaptation of existing structures.

1.7a

The broch is delicately constructed from varying sizes of dry stone.

1.7b

The concentric circular structure is clearly visible amongst the ruin.

1.7a

Preservation

Name: Dun Telve and Dun Troddan Brochs
Location: Glenelg, UK

Preservation is a practice that maintains the building or structure in its found state, however ruinous that may be. The building is made safe and any further decay is prevented from occurring; the ruined condition is important to the historical understanding of the place.

An extraordinary example of preserved structures is the series of brochs built about 2,000 years ago in the north of Scotland. Brochs are tall stone towers, up to about 8 meters (26 feet) high. Built from two concentric circles of dry stone, they were both defensive and protective. The gap between the walls provided sufficient space for living, sleeping, and circulation, possibly with different wooden floor levels within the structure, while the ground level center area was probably used for the animals. The building was most likely to have had a timber roof. These structures have been preserved in their ruinous state, the possibility of any further decay has been prevented, but no attempt to return them to their original condition has been made.

Society for the Protection of Ancient Buildings

William Morris founded the Society for the Protection of Ancient Buildings (SPAB) in 1877. The society's aims are to preserve and repair buildings, with respect to their age and character. They regard the romance and authenticity of the building as important and advise on the methods and skills necessary to retain this.

1.7b

Restoration

Name: Villa Savoye
Location: Poissy, France
Designer: Le Corbusier

Restoration is the process of returning the condition of the building to its original state, and this often involves using materials and techniques of the original period to ensure that the building appears as it would have when constructed. This type of approach is typically used to conserve precious or listed buildings such as churches and other historic buildings, where the method of occupying them has not drastically changed. One of the most obvious problems with this approach is that historic buildings have often been added to, changed, or substantially altered, during their history and so there is a question as to which of these states the building should be restored to.

Another important consideration is the reason for the restoration. For what purpose is the building to be restored? Is it so that it can remain within the collective memory as a reminder of where we have come from? Or, will that leave it useless and unfit for any modern use?

A typical example of this type of project is Le Corbusier's modernist masterpiece, Villa Savoye. It was originally constructed in 1929 as a weekend country home, but it now stands as a monument to the five points of architecture: free façade, free plan, pilotis or columns, active roof space, and horizontal windows. It is now little more than a museum of architectural promenade.

The Venice Charter

The International Charter for the Conservation and Restoration of Monuments and Sites (The Venice Charter, 1964) is a document that gives an international framework for the preservation and restoration of ancient buildings. The intention of the charter is to safeguard these sites as both works of art and as historical evidence.

1.8

The Villa Savoye after it had been restored.

"Most of the work on older buildings affects their interiors. Not only must designers or architects be competent with current code requirements, structural realities, mechanical and electrical services, and economic restrictions, but they must be knowledgeable of architectural and social history."

John Kurtich & Garrett Eakin

Renovation

Name: The Rookery
Location: Chicago, USA
Designer: T. Gunny Harboe

Renovation is the process of renewing and updating a building. The function will remain the same and the structure is generally untouched, but the manner in which the building is used will be brought up to date. It is usually the services that require attention, especially the heating and sanitary systems. A good example of refurbishment is a large mansion that will be adapted for twenty-first-century living but not substantially changed.

The renovation of the court lobby of the Rookery was a complex process of balancing the conservation of the original 1888 building with several previous renovations of the building and the needs of the present users. The narrative of the journey through the eleven-story, cast-iron frame masonry and terracotta office block by original architects, Burnham & Root, had been compromised by the progressive alterations, as had the natural light through the glass roof and the vertical circulation. The 1905 renovation by Frank Lloyd Wright continued the spatial journey through the building and clad the cast-iron columns with white marble. Gunny Harboe was anxious to embrace this work, while erasing the subsequent alterations, so a datum of 1910 was set. The original circulation route was re-established, the entrance vestibule was restored to Wright's design, and Burnham & Root's original marble mosaic floor was rebuilt. Most importantly, a new glazed roof was built above the original, which eliminated any problems of water ingress and reinstated the former brilliantly lit courtyard. This whole process adapted the building for twenty-first-century expectations and use.

1.9a

1.9a

The vertical circulation of the Rookery was clearly defined in the renovation.

1.9b

The renovation makes the priory once again fit for purpose.

1.9b

1.10a

1.10a

The exhibits are carefully positioned within each individual gallery to encourage movement through the space, and from one room to another.

Remodeling

Name: Castelvecchio Museum
Location: Verona, Italy
Designer: Carlo Scarpa

Remodeling is the process of wholeheartedly altering a building. The function is the most obvious change, but other alterations may be made to the building itself, such as the circulation route, the orientation, and the relationships between spaces. Additions or extensions may be constructed, while other areas may be demolished. This process is sometimes referred to as adaptive reuse, especially in the USA, or as reworking, adaptation, interior architecture, or even interior design.

Carlo Scarpa was, essentially, the forerunner of an approach based upon a sympathetic understanding of the existing building and he is still considered the greatest exponent of the art of remodeling. His masterpiece, the Castelvecchio Museum in Verona, is composed of a complex of buildings, courtyards, gardens, and the tower of the Scaliger Castle. It is situated beside a bridge that spans the River Adige, which runs through the center of Verona.

The approach taken by Scarpa was one based upon an interpretation of the meaning of the original building. He endeavored to understand the historical and contextual qualities of the place and then applied a new contemporary layer of value and consequence to the building. In response to the three main periods of the castle's history, the layers of building were scraped away and exposed, until the junctions where time was most obvious, were revealed. A new layer of small, beautifully composed additions were then imposed upon the building, a layer that expressed the contemporary nature of their design, but which was totally appropriate and sympathetic to the original building.

Carlo Scarpa

Scarpa regarded himself as belonging to the Italian tradition of working with existing buildings, often citing the example of Brunelleschi, whose masterpiece, the dome of the Duomo in Florence, Italy, was an addition to an existing building.

1.10b

1.10b

The open latticework screen is deliberately just half-opened to encourage diagonal movement through the gallery.

2.1

2 The Existing Building

The most significant difference between the design of interiors and the design of almost anything else is the existence of the original building. The interior designer has to be forever conscious of the continual presence of an existing structure. However, far from this being a handicap or constraining factor, it can be used as a valuable tool, an instrument of liberation. In the process of creating interior space, through the reworking of the existing building or given space, the stimulus for transformation can often be found in the existing building. This section will explain how the elements of the redesign can respond to the stimulus of the reading or analysis of the structure and rhythm of the existing building. The different methods of establishing a relationship between the new and old will be outlined and the significance of the important theory of remodeling, "Form follows form," will be discussed.

2.1

Name: Churchgate House
Location: Manchester, UK
Designer: Atelier MB, in collaboration with Space Invader

Introduction

Reading the interior

Careful analysis of the space can offer many clues and pointers to the redesign. Understanding the plan, section, and elevations of the building or space allows the designer to explore the relationships between the qualities of a space and its subsequent adaptation to a new use.

Basic structural systems

Thorough knowledge of structural issues can communicate the most practical methods of conversion and change, and avoid potentially dangerous construction problems. Rhythm, form, and visual balance can also influence the subsequent issues of the remodeling.

Context and environment

All buildings have their own individual context and there are many considerations, both inside and outside, that can be manipulated and shaped within the reorganization. Environmental issues need to be considered, not just problems of solar gain, or stopping the rain from getting in, but also questions of the impact of any design upon the natural world.

History

An analysis of the existing building can expose features that may not be immediately discernible. Buildings evolve and develop over time; their original function will have determined their shape and form, their structural logic, and their outward appearance. The previous users of the building will have affected its character—indeed, if it was designed for a particular use, then it will have a specific organization. The new use may be completely different to their original purpose, yet an analysis of these features, their changes over time, and their new functional requirements are important considerations. The analysis of growth and changes throughout the history of the building can offer some interesting clues to reuse.

Form follows form

It is through the understanding of the pre-existing that the remodeled building can become endowed with a new and greater meaning. An investigation of the archaeology of the original can reveal previously hidden or obsolete characteristics that contain the possibility of being exploited: the place can be activated.

2.2

St Paul's Church, London

New meets old in the interior of St Paul's Church, Bow, UK.

Reading the Interior

The reading of an existing building is a process that can be conducted in a series of methodical and distinct ways. This section will look at a number of analytical processes that the designer can adopt in order to understand the existing space.

Reading the plan

Name: Marienkirche and Library
Location: Muncheberg, Germany
Designer: Klaus Block

The drawn outline of a space or building indicates the parameters of the space to be used in the new design. This is described as the plan of the existing structure: it can be the meticulous survey of an existing building or a drawing of an as yet unbuilt structure. Understanding the extent of the plan of a space is an important part of the interior design process, as the drawing will indicate not only the exact area to be designed, but it can also provide information about the nature of the original building.

The reading of a plan of the existing building, or new space, can give clues to the distribution and nature of the function (both previous and proposed): the organization, the structure, and the rhythm of a space. Contextual features such as bays, windows, and doorways are indicated in the drawings. The site plan also shows how the space or building is situated within its context. This drawing will indicate such factors as orientation, aspect, the relationship with neighboring buildings, roads, and public spaces. This type of information is not always possible to fathom when visiting the site, and is near impossible if the building is

unbuilt. It is these details that can give clues to the designer and influence the transformation of the space. The reading of the surrounding envelope of the existing building has directly influenced the restoration in 1994 of the Marienkirche in Muncheberg, Germany, and the planning of the new town library. The body of the existing church was clearly organized into two distinct areas: the nave and the chancel. The congregation had dwindled, so when the opportunity to combine the secular with the spiritual arose, it was obvious how the building should be split. The church retained the chancel and the library took over the nave. However, it was important that the two activities did not interfere with each other. The library is housed in an elegant timber and glass structure, reminiscent of the hull of a boat moored within the cavernous nave of the church. It is separated, both visually and acoustically, from the congregation, who pass through the space around the library to get to their seats. A free-standing lift services the library, clad with dark gray steel mesh, and perhaps seen as a modern interpretation of the Marienkirche's bell tower; an eighteenth-century addition by Karl Friedrich Schinkel.

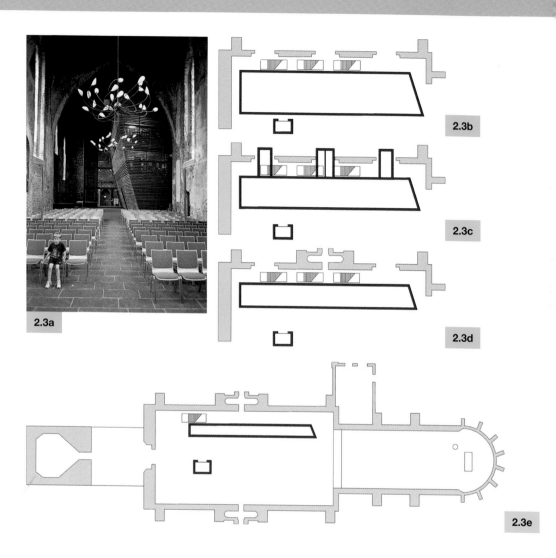

2.3a

2.3b

2.3c

2.3d

2.3e

2.3a

View of the library from the chancel.

2.3b

Third floor plan.

2.3c

Second floor plan.

2.3d

First floor plan.

2.3e

Ground floor plan.

Reading the section

Name: Fourth Church of Christ Scientist
Location: Manchester, UK
Designer: OMI Architects

At any point on the plan of a building, the designer may describe a line through the drawing and visualize a vertical cut through the spaces. This is called a section and it will explain the volumes of the spaces and indicate the position of the walls, the floors, the roof, and other structural elements. The building or space to be designed or reused can be read as a series of spaces and levels within an enclosure, and this understanding allows the designer to respond to the existing forms and volumes. This type of drawing also allows the designer to investigate such issues as an exploration of the structure, the admission of light, vertical interaction within the building, and relationships between the interior and the exterior.

The section allowed OMI to understand the volumetric properties of a banal office block in Manchester. Without this collection of drawings, they would not have been able to visually analyze the building so thoroughly, as complex three-dimensional relationships are not always obvious to the naked eye. This examination led the designers to carve from deep within the lower floors of the building a triple-height chapel. This large room or volume is surrounded by circulation space, through which shines natural light. At ground floor level, at the front of the building, the designers manipulated the barely double-height space to accommodate a reception and bookshop with a tiny reading room. A series of sections through the building provided the architects with a greater understanding of the building, and this placed them in a position to develop complex relationships within the space.

"Every place has its datum-line, and one may be on it or above it or below it."

Gordon Cullen

2.4a

Section through the church. The space appears to be carved from the heart of the existing building.

2.4b

Concept sketch of the church interior.

2.4c

The structure of the existing building is emphasized to produce a subtle reference for the spiritual space.

2.4d

The message of the space is framed in the interior.

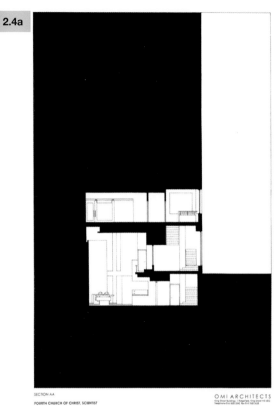

SECTION AA

FOURTH CHURCH OF CHRIST, SCIENTIST

OMI ARCHITECTS

2.4a

2.4b

2.4c

2.4d

God
is
love

Reading the elevation

Name: Sir John Soane's Museum
Location: London, UK
Designer: Sir John Soane

The façade of a building usually refers to the front elevation; it typically means the vertical element of a building that has direct relationship with the street. The façade will normally show the position of the entrance, communicate the organization of the interior spaces, depict the patterns and volumes of the activities behind it, and establish links with other structures nearby. Obviously not all elevations perform these tasks, there are many examples, particularly of contemporary buildings that do not even have what could commonly be described as a façade.

Sir John Soane's Museum (1804) is an enchanting collection of exquisite spaces and rooms enclosed by carefully manipulated walls of extreme depth and articulation. The organization of these spaces represents that type of inhabitation that was prevalent in the late eighteenth and early nineteenth centuries. The front elevation of the building is remarkably plain and calm compared with the complex density of the interior; however, it is equally ingenious. The building was once the family home of the Soane family, and was remodeled from two fairly plain Georgian terraced townhouses. Soane chose to differentiate the primary dwelling from the rest of the street by attaching an extension to the front of the building. This manifests itself on the exterior of the building as a projecting loggia or gallery, and within the interior as the privacy of a thickened out wall that contains books, ornaments, and pictures. The family could stand at their first floor windows and commune directly with the street, or retreat to the security of the recess or alcove for a discrete conversation.

2.5a

2.5a

This cutaway model, constructed from gray cardboard, shows the articulation of the layers of the façade.

2.5b

The façade of the museum consists of a new element placed immediately in front of the original elevation. This screen wall creates an identity for the building and distinguishes it from the rest of the terrace of townhouses.

2.5b

"The façade…talks about the cultural situation at the time when the building was built."

Rob Krier

Three-dimensional form

Name: German Museum of Architecture
Location: Frankfurt, Germany
Designer: O.M. Ungers

The plan, section, and elevation of a building can all be read together to provide information about the three-dimensional qualities of the building. The plan will show the extent of a space, while the section will show the height, and combined they will indicate the volume. These orthographic drawings are diagrams that aid the designer's understanding of a building or space, but it is the three-dimensional qualities that are seen, felt, heard, and experienced. From this analysis, the volume and form can be established and subsequently considered in the design process.

Frankfurt has pursued a policy of regeneration through culture by redeveloping the south bank of the river Main with a series of museums. As part of this development, O.M. Ungers has created an extraordinary museum within the confines of an existing building. The modest exterior of the neoclassical townhouse has been wrapped with an equally reserved single-story, red sandstone colonnade; but it is within the museum that the true extent of the remodeling can be experienced. Ungers has inserted a huge white representation of a house into the cleared interior of the building—"a house within a house." This element controls and defines the extent of the exhibitions and can be accessed from every floor. A powerful three-dimensional grid defines the position and size of the house. From the entrance hall, four columns direct the eye upwards and the sheer size of this clean, white element is obvious through the void of the empty space. It is a very powerful gesture, a post-modern, almost ironic symbol of architecture.

"it would be difficult to name any internationally recognized architect without making a reference to their drawing style."

Tom Porter

2.6a

2.6a

The modest neoclassical exterior has been sensitively altered.

2.6b

2.6b

A house within a house.

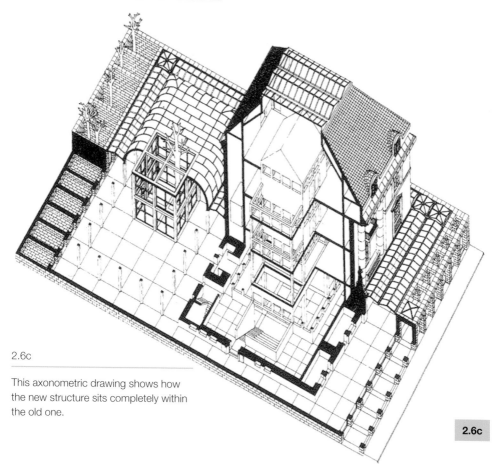

2.6c

This axonometric drawing shows how the new structure sits completely within the old one.

2.6c

Basic Structural Systems

This section will examine the different basic structural systems and the types of interior that can be created from them. It will examine the qualities of interiors designed as a result of understanding and using these systems.

What is structure?

Structure can be described as a collection or assemblage of materials that, when joined together, will withstand the loads and forces to which they are subjected. These loads are not confined just to the weight of the building itself, but will also include such forces as wind, people, furniture, and fittings. The interior designer needs to have an understanding of structure in order to be sure that any alterations or additions that they make to an existing building will not compromise its structural integrity.

Up until the end of the twentieth century, there were two basic methods of construction: load bearing and frame. The load-bearing structure is thick and heavy, and is usually constructed from bricks or stone blocks built up from the ground. This type of structure generally creates small confined spaces due to the restricted span of the roof or floor beams, and the windows are of a limited size. The frame structure is constructed from a series of columns and beams, usually organized in a grid formation, which take the weight of the building. They can be made from concrete, steel, or timber. This creates large open spaces. The walls, which take no structural load, can be divorced from the structure and so the choice of cladding material is almost unlimited. This type of organization is referred to as "free-plan." The twenty-first century has brought contemporary methods of construction, such as monocoques and fractals, and has seen the resurgence of barrel vaulting.

The structural logic of an existing building is a key factor that will influence the remodeling. Different types and qualities of space can be created from different structural systems. This understanding is a key part of the reading and analysis of the building.

2.7

The steel-framed restaurant and shops are inserted into the brick and timber structure of the Great Butchers' Hall (Groentenmarkt) in Ghent, Belgium.

Load-bearing structures

Name: Scottish Poetry Library
Location: Edinburgh, UK
Designer: Malcolm Fraser Architects

Load-bearing buildings contain thick walls, constructed using stone or brick, and are built up from the ground, layer by layer, incorporating their own weight. The organization of the building and its spaces can be very random, although there is a constraint upon the size of the spaces created; they can be positioned without any considerations for order, rhythm, or control. There is generally a limit to the height of the building: the walls at the base become ridiculously wide should the building become too high. The restriction upon the volume of the individual rooms is caused by the difficulty of spanning the space; wood and steel beams are generally of a limited length. Victorian buildings combined cast-iron columns with brick outer walls to accommodate the need for large uninterrupted spaces.

Openings in the walls have to ensure that they do not compromise the structural integrity of the building, so they tend to be quite small and aligned. The top is supported by an arch or lintel.

The reuse of load-bearing buildings usually results in a very specific type of interior architecture: small confined spaces with relatively restricted natural light. Any structural changes have to be thoroughly compensated for. This was the most common building technique before the nineteenth century and, as a consequence, will often be the subject of a remodeling project. The Scottish Poetry Library is partially built upon the old city wall that surrounded Edinburgh. It uses the wall as a protective container that also supports the roof at the rear of the library. The front of the building is a modern steel, timber, and glass construction. The original arrow slit eyelet windows of the city wall illuminate the gaps between the bookshelves, thus a book is selected from the protective shadowy depths of the building and brought into the light.

2.8a

Books are selected within the depths of the building.

2.8b

This sectional perspective shows how the building sits on the city wall at the back and opens up to the landscape at the front.

2.8c

The open-stepped terrace for reading is clearly visible at the front of the building.

2.8a

2.8b

2.8c

Malcolm Fraser Architects

Malcolm Fraser Architects are recognized for their sympathetic and contextual approach to architecture and the remodeling of buildings in sensitive and historic environments. As well as the Scottish Poetry Library, they have successfully reused buildings for Dance Base and the Scottish Storytelling Centre.

Frame

Name: La Llauna School
Location: Barcelona, Spain
Designer: Enric Miralles and Carme Pinós

A building with a frame construction usually has a definite order to it. The columns are generally arranged as a grid, leaving free, uninterrupted space between them. The frame is usually made from steel, concrete, or timber. The floors are generally in-filled between the beams of the frame and, as such, they will have a limited ability to take weight. When Jakob and Macfarlane designed the Restaurant Georges in the Pompidou Centre (see page 140), they had to be very conscious of the thin concrete slab floors.

The walls within and surrounding the building can be thin, as they do not have to correspond to the frame; this is described as "free-plan." They can be arranged into any pattern or organization that will support the activity of the building. The choice of material for the internal walls and cladding is also almost unlimited. They only have to support themselves; they take no structural load and so can be constructed with consideration to other factors, such as acoustic control, visual impact, or organization. The external walls, or cladding, are also non-structural, but environmental control will be an important factor in their design. Keeping the rain out, preventing excessive solar gain,

and providing acoustic and visual privacy are important considerations. However, this is not always the case: Blur Pavilion, designed by Diller Scofidio + Renfro for the 2002 Expo in Switzerland, is still cited, almost a generation after its installation, as having the most radical of façades; the architects proposed the use of steam from hundreds of sprinklers to surround and define the building.

For La Llauna School, Miralles and Pinós used the structural logic of a disused printing warehouse to inform the organization of the new school that was placed within it. The classrooms, staff rooms, circulation, and even the playground are positioned with consideration for the steel frame structure. A series of architectural interventions were slipped between the structure; the stairs rise through a vertical slot of space and open a route through the building; classrooms are placed in-between the grid of columns, and at ground level, all superfluous elements have been stripped away to leave just the frame, thus creating an open yet sheltered area for the children's playground. The small school, built on an incredibly constrained site, is an elegant and distinct conversation between new and old.

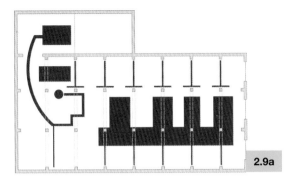

2.9a

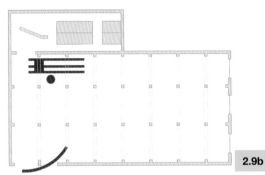

2.9b

2.9a–2.9b

First floor and ground floor plans.

2.9c

The frame of the building dictates the position of the stairs.

2.9d

The rhythm of the building structure is visible on the top floor, which is awaiting remodeling.

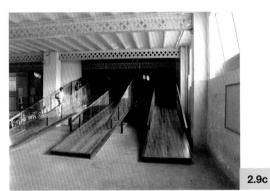

2.9c

2.9d

Unusual structures

Name: ING & NNH Head Offices
Location: Budapest, Hungary
Designer: Erick van Egeraat (EEA)

As well as straightforward frame and load-bearing structure systems, there is a more unusual method of construction. With the advent of three-dimensional modeling software, designers can now create seamless structures that combine the walls, floors, and the roof of a building.

The fractal geometries of Frank Gehry and Daniel Libeskind produce complex geometries that twist and turn to produce contorted interior spaces. Monocoque constructions, such as the media centre at Lord's cricket ground in London designed by Future Systems, are similar in construction to the hulls of boats and distort the usual relationships between floors, walls, and ceilings. Digital modeling can create forms that are impossible to draw by hand, the complex curves and awkward forms created through parametric or digitally modeled architecture has been nicknamed "Blobitecture" for obvious reasons. (See Zaha Hadid Maxxi page 125.)

Eric van Egeraat has added a dramatic and provocative element to a sober neo-Renaissance building that was designed in 1882 in the center of Budapest. The orthogonal five-story building is arranged around a full height courtyard, and is elegantly ordered with cast-iron balconies and windows. The protected building was painstakingly restored, any lost details of the ornament were reconstructed, and the destroyed and damaged fabric was cleaned and repaired. It was important that any new additions were not visible from the street, so accordingly, it was within the courtyard that the insertion was placed.

Set into the roof of the building and hovering over the courtyard is a new double-height structure with a translucent green glass underside. Known locally as "the whale," this large monocoque construction functions as a viewing platform and meeting room. Egeraat describes the strategy as "modern baroque," prioritizing the roof or ceiling of a space and ensuring that the visitor looks up as they enter: "In that modern baroque, it is essential to leave symmetry and structure behind and instead introduce asymmetry and disharmony, freed from its negative connotations. I am above all obsessed with the excitement one feels in all that is indefinable and inexplicable."[1]

[1] Van Egeraat, E. 1997. *EEA Six Ideas about Architecture*. New York: Birkhäuser

2.10a

2.10b

2.10c

2.10a

"The whale" sits on top of the roof of the neo-Renaissance building.

2.10b

The meeting room emerges from its glass surrounds.

2.10c

The enigmatic space of the boardroom inside "the whale".

2.11a

Rhythm

Name: Alte Pinakothek
Location: Munich, Germany
Designer: Hans Döllgast

The structural system of a building can help create an order or rhythm. This may be little more than a sequence of identical windows, or perhaps an ornate covered colonnade. A procession of repeated elements can tie long buildings together and can also compensate for any discrepancies within the building. Palladio used a rhythm of columns and arches to wrap around the Basilica in Vicenza, Italy (see page 156). This acted to conceal the distorted shape of the interior building.

The Alte Pinakothek was designed in 1836 by Leo von Klenze as part of King Ludwig I of Bavaria's ambition to turn Munich into the Venice of the North. The central section of the neoclassical building was destroyed during the Second World War. The design for the restoration of the Pinakothek was not only modern, but also it also managed to reflect the rhythm and tempo of the original building. The 19-meter high (62 feet) brick piers that had been destroyed were replaced with 250 mm (nine and a half inches) circular steel columns. New sections of the roof were formed in aluminum and the brick wall was reinstated, but in a more simple and austere manner. This gives the foyer space a minimal and modern quality, while the remodeling of the exterior appears to be appropriate without resorting to pastiche.

Döllgast appreciated that the building had a history, and he felt it important to recognize and respect this. The reinstatement of the rhythm and order of the original building ensured that there was a direct connection between the new and the old.

Hans Döllgast

Hans Döllgast (1891–1974) was much admired for his inventive use of modernist principles in the conservation of historic buildings. As well as the Pinakothek, he designed two modern roof structures for war-damaged churches in Munich, St Bonifaz and Allerheilgenhof. Both structures are sympathetic to the existing building and yet are still modern and uncompromising.

2.11a

The repaired section is celebrated. The rhythm of the old dictates the new.

2.11b

The difference between the language of the old and the new is clearly visible at the point at which they meet.

2.11b

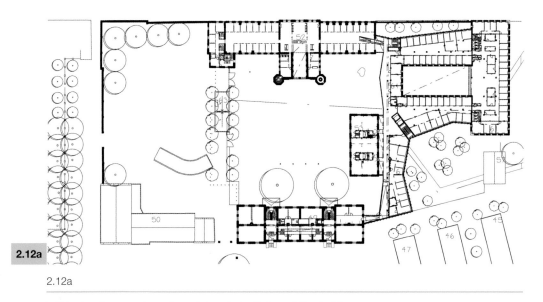

2.12a

2.12a

In this plan, the new elements are integrated with the existing buildings.

Form/balance

Name: Norwegian Ministry of Defence
Location: Oslo, Norway
Designer: Jarmund/Vigsnæs AS Arkitekter MNAL

Both the proximity and characteristics of an extant building can often be used to either harmonize or counterpoint a new construction or element. Rather than a constraining factor, the presence of an existing structure can enhance innovation and be a valuable tool to be used as inspiration in the creative processes of designing a new interior or building.

The designers of the new Norwegian Ministry of Defence have carefully combined a series of protected existing buildings with a set of contemporary transparent and solid structures. The new buildings needed to incorporate a series of existing structures on the site, to form a strong perimeter to the eastern side of the Akershus Fortress in Oslo, whilst also increasing the connections between the departments of the Ministry.

The workshop of the fortress provided a counterpoint for a new glazed courtyard structure that connected to a new office block. Clad in a dark engineering brick, it was reminiscent of the arsenal of the fortress. A glazed wing linking old and new was set back from a retained wall, part of a nineteenth-century plan by Schirmer and Von Hanno. The variety in style, material, and their proportions of the existing buildings were utilized in order to provide clear distinctions and balance between new and old, exemplifying an ongoing dialogue between the past and the future.

The cuts and abrasions of the original building are carefully enclosed and exhibited behind glass.

2.12b

"Architectural design is always carried into effect by means of dimensions and the way in which they may be repeated and grouped in order to establish controlled relationships between them."

Pierre von Meiss

Context and Environment

"Context and Environment" examines the impact that the surroundings of a building can have upon its redesign. It also discusses such environmental considerations as topography and light.

Context: Site

Name: CCCB (Centre de Cultura Contemporánia de Barcelona)
Location: Barcelona, Spain
Designer: Albert Viaplana, Helio Piñon

The exterior context around an interior can be an important and influential consideration. There are many site-specific situations that influence the shape and form of a building, and subsequently have an effect on the design of its interior. Such contextual factors can include aspect, orientation, topography, the patterns of streets and roads, urban density, and the relationship with a significant landmark.

The CCCB is housed in an elegant eighteenth-century building arranged around a courtyard. Around three sides of the courtyard, the Casa de Caritat (the Almshouse), a four-story building with basements, was retained, and on the fourth side the building was demolished and a new

insertion was placed within this gap. It was built to fit, adhering to the exact plan dimensions of its predecessor. The courtyard façade of the new building is a striking glazed screen that is angled at the top as it rises over the rooftops of the other buildings. The main circulation routes are secreted behind this screen, but it is in front of it that the most significant moment of the building is discovered. The glazed screen is highly reflective, offering mirror images of the buildings and the courtyard. However, when the visitor is positioned upon a specific bench on the far side of the courtyard, the angled screen provides a view over the roofscape to the sea. Immediately, a relationship is established with things both close up and far away.

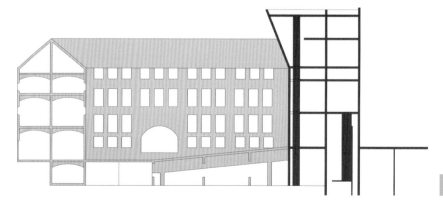

2.13a

2.13b

2.13a

This section through the courtyard shows how the screen defines the fourth edge of the courtyard.

2.13b

Old meets new where the screen is inserted into the courtyard.

2.13c

The world beyond the courtyard is reflected in the angled screen.

2.13c

"The relationship between the object and the intervening spaces is not formal: it is always rooted in the context of a particular setting."

Dalibor Vesely

2.14a

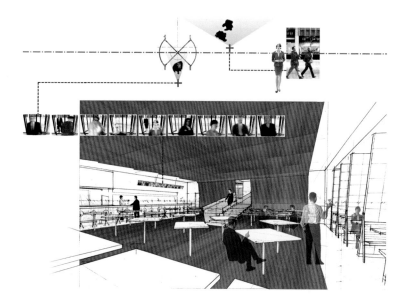

Context: Exterior

Name: The Brasserie
Location: New York, USA
Designer: Diller + Scofidio

Important contextual factors do not only shape the exterior of the building but can also exert great influence upon the interior. Although the location, scale, size, and shape of an existing building can influence the reuse, psychological factors can also have a significant effect.

Ludwig Mies van der Rohe designed the Seagram Building in New York in 1959. It is the archetypical international style building, a symbol of modernity's obsession with right angles, overt structure, and truth to materials. This is expressed in the sleek curtain wall of smoked glass and the exposed bronze structure. The Seagram was notable for the fact that it did not fill its expansive Park Avenue lot to the perimeter. Instead, the architect set the building back from the road on a travertine plinth, almost a piece of sculpture set apart from its neighbors. Within the basement of the plinth

was the fashionable Four Seasons Restaurant. This was designed by Philip Johnson, who was exclusively and extensively responsible for everything, right down to the napkins. After a very destructive fire, the restaurant was remodeled by Diller + Scofidio in 2000.

The context provoked a response based upon the contradictions of the immediate environment: a basement location without a view of the outside world, which was situated in the bottom of an iconic example of transparency and light. Therefore, the Brasserie is conceived around the concept, of watching and being watched. Diners are observed twice: firstly, upon entrance their image is relayed to one of a series of screens suspended above the bar and then again, when they enter the catwalk-type staircase into the dining area—an experience that is not for the shy or fainthearted.

2.14b

2.14c

2.14d

2.14a

A concept sketch of the interior.

2.14b

The space is conceived as a series of eating and drinking experiences.

2.14c

Images of the visitors are displayed on screens above the bar.

2.14d

The restaurant is located within the basement plinth of the Seagram plaza.

Philip Johnson

Philip Johnson (1906–2005) was one of the twentieth century's most influential architects. His early career included working with a number of eminent modernist architects, including Mies van der Rohe, Le Corbusier, and Walter Gropius. His own masterpiece, the Glass House (1949) was a composition in minimalism and transparency. In a complete rejection of this style, he designed, in 1984, what has been described as the first post-modern building, the AT&T Building.

Context: Artificial light

Name: St Martins Lane Hotel
Location: London, UK
Designer: Philippe Starck

Artificial light can be regarded as a material with definite properties that can be refined and manipulated. The artist James Turrell has created a series of installations, all of which exploit the deceptive possibilities that bright light, and its opposite, extreme dark, can offer. Artificial light is of course most visible at night, or in a space undisturbed by natural light.

In the heart of London's West End, a 1960s' modernist block, the former home of a major advertising agency, has been transformed to become an exclusive boutique hotel. Within the interior, Starck employs his usual wit in the design of a post-modern collection of magnified and classically inspired furniture. Each space is radically different, the Light Bar is vivid and brightly colored, and the lobby is cool, spacious and white, with a 10-foot high vase of flowers and massive representations of gold teeth and corks acting as cocktail chairs and tables. The Asia de Cuba & Rum Bar contains a tight grid of tiny tables tottering on tall slender legs, and the outrageously large columns in the restaurant are enclosed with bookshelves and picture walls—an ironic interpretation of the family living room?

However, Starck reserves his most extravagant gesture for the exterior of the building. The outside walls of the fairly anonymous office block have a visible structural concrete grid, and floor to ceiling glazing. Starck exploits this transparency: by day, the hotel retains its undistinguished character, but at night each room glows with colored light and thus the building is transformed into a bright and glowing patchwork. The guests control the color and intensity of the light, they can select the color that they feel most reflects their emotion, offering the passing pedestrian a hint of what is happening behind the net curtains.

2.15a

"Light is not so much something that reveals, as it is itself the revelation."
James Turrell

2.15a

By day, the building is undistinguished.

2.15b

2.15d

2.15c

2.15e

2.15b

By night, the façade is animated through light.

2.15c

Idiosyncratic furniture and enigmatic objects are crammed into the foyer space.

2.15d

Vivid colored light illuminates the space in the Light Bar.

2.15e

Color and atmosphere is created in the restaurant by the columns, which have been wrapped with bookshelves.

History

The history of an existing building can be analyzed and the findings can influence the subsequent redesign. This section will examine the use of history as a transformative tool in the redesign process.

History: Study 1

Name: 192 Shoreham Street
Location: Sheffield, UK
Designer: Project Orange

Buildings are generally constructed for a specific purpose, and the organization as well as the form of the original structure are designed in a way to accommodate that particular use. This means that the previous function of a building can have a significant impact upon the nature of the new design. Remnants of the earlier lives will be present within the body of the structure because buildings are engrained with the stories and histories of the people who use them. Rodolfo Machado likens this to the palimpsest, which is the act of reusing and writing over a parchment or animal skin; inevitably, remnants of past inscriptions interrupt the clarity of the next incarnation. This relationship between the prevailing and the proposed provides the designer with the opportunity to reflect upon the contingency, usefulness, and emotional resonance of existing places and structures.

Sheffield has a significant industrial history, indeed it earned the sobriquet "Steel City" due to the sheer quantity of the material that was manufactured there in the nineteenth and twentieth centuries. The city also had a reputation for high-quality silversmithing, and numerous small works developed during that period along the River Sheaf. Many of these now-redundant buildings are situated in the newly formed Cultural Industries Quarter of the city. 192 Shoreham Street is a significant industrial structure that has been remodeled by Project Orange to accommodate a mixture of offices and restaurants. Project Orange created an enormous floating roof structure that is reminiscent of the industrial roofscapes that used to dominate the city. This allows the interior to accommodate a double height restaurant space with more compact but open offices above. The remodeled building acts as both a symbol of the industrial history of the city and a beacon to its future.

2.16a

2.16c

2.16b

2.16a

The simple industrial character of the original building is reflected in the new elements of reuse.

2.16b

The dramatic new roofscape of the building is a direct reference to the industrial past of the city.

2.16c

The plywood clad interior circulation area reflects the robust character of the industrial building.

History: Study 2

Name: Rivoli Museum of Contemporary Art
Location: Rivoli, near Turin, Italy
Designer: Andrea Bruno Architects

A building can evolve, but it can retain a remembrance of its former function and value; it has a memory of its previous purpose ingrained within its very structure. The exploitation and development of this can create a composite of meaning and consequence. The inherent qualities of the place and its surroundings, combined with the anticipation of the future use, produce a multi-layered complexity impossible to replicate in a new building. The study or analysis of individual structures is almost an archaeological investigation. The history and changing function of a building is a valuable narrative that can be analyzed and then used in the transformation process.

Andrea Bruno was commissioned to convert the Castello di Rivoli (which had originally been built for the Savoy family by Filippo Juvarra) into the Museum of Contemporary Art. His careful and thorough analysis of the site revealed not one building, but several distinct layers of buildings from different eras. The elegant but unfinished eighteenth-century house was built upon the ruins of a seventeenth-century palace that had been constructed on top of a sixteenth-century castle, which itself was built over medieval ruins. Each layer was not fully demolished before the successive building was constructed, hence Bruno discovered that the site contained half of an eighteenth-century palace, an incredibly long seventeenth-century picture gallery and just some remains of the older buildings.

Bruno's approach was to celebrate this diversity and to stitch these individual and distinctive elements together with a series of obviously modern interventions. Apart from the new roof for the picture gallery, the additions facilitated movement through and around the site. This encouraged the visitor to examine the buildings

with the same scrutiny as the art. No attempt was made to physically connect the buildings, but a small balcony was cantilevered from the chateau to provide a visual link, thus allowing the visitor to make their own connection. Bruno has thus created another layer of archaeology that ties together the collage of the museum.

2.17a

2.17a

The viewing balcony projects from the original building.

2.17b

The new stairs are inserted into the old stairwell.

"when the organizational geometries do not reside in the objects themselves, the possibilities of combining various buildings within a system of order which attributes to each piece a bit of the organization become almost infinite."

Thomas Schumacher

Form Follows Form

There are many methods of adapting old buildings for new uses. The qualities found within the existing can be a highly influential factor within the redesign process. The form of the existing can inform the form of the new.

Form follows form: Study 1

Name: St Paul's Church, Bow
Location: London, UK
Designer: Matthew Lloyd Architects

When a building is renewed or remodeled, the most important consideration is the nature of that building. For the design to be both sympathetic and appropriate, the designer must be able to appreciate the qualities of the existing construct. The shape and appearance of the building will inevitably influence the form of the new interior, because it is itself the material that is to be altered and shaped.

The church at Bow is a collection of assorted elements gathered together in one building. It is modestly gothic (1878), with a cylindrical three-story bell tower, very large pointed windows and clerestory lights and an open nave. The ceiling over the chancel is highly decorated, the gold ribs run into the cast-iron columns, which are positioned centrally in front of pilasters between the windows. It appears that the brick walls of the nave were once painted white, but these have been allowed to peel and fade. The pews are placed around the raised altar and the organ is positioned against a blocked up arch. Into this mixture, Matthew Lloyd Architects have inserted a two-story steel and timber structure. It is raised high into the vaulted ceiling of the church to leave the chancel and the nave free for worship.

The front of this bold, curved wooden structure is supported by four enormous white-painted Y-shaped steel columns, which just stand among the pews. The rear is connected to a white rectangular box of a quite different nature, and contained within this is the meeting room and stairs to the gallery, gym, and community rooms at first and second levels. The building has been split three-dimensionally into two L-shaped sections. The church occupies the L at the front and ground level, and the community uses the L at the top and back of the building. The language of the new is quite different to that of the old, but then each area is an assemblage of different styles, components, and functions, the solution of which seems to work.

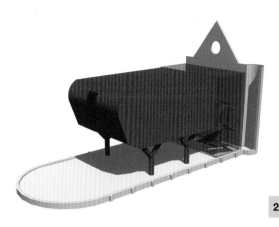

2.18a

2.18a

Three-dimensional drawing of the new insertion and the old building.

2.18b

Plan of the project.

2.18c

The new insertion is squeezed into the nave of the church.

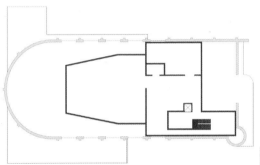

2.18b

2.18c

2.19a

2.19a

The crisp, white, new insertion derives its formal inspiration from the unrelenting frame of the concrete structure.

Form follows form: Study 2

Name: Daxing Factory Conversion
Location: Beijing, China
Designer: Nie Yong and Yoshimasa Tsutsumi

Inspiration can be acquired from any existing space that a designer will reuse. Whether a distinguished building, full of character, or a construction lacking any unique features, a thorough comprehension of the qualities of the host space is crucial. This can then lead to a deeper and more substantial meaning for the new interior.

An existing building with an unprepossessing character, constructed with an unrelenting structural grid, was remodeled to become the new headquarters for the Daxing Furniture Company. The lower floors of the building were designed to accommodate the production side of the business. The upper floors were to become the offices of the company. The synergy between the two elements of the business was important to maintain, yet high-quality, upper-level workspaces and showrooms were required in order to present a distinct outward appearance to clients and workers alike.

The square form of the building was constructed utilizing a concrete frame. The two upper floors of the building were treated as a double-height geometric interior landscape. The uniform grid of the concrete structure was translated into an orthogonal planned frame consisting of a series of open and enclosed spaces. The open spaces accommodate accessible areas, such as exhibition and circulation. The enclosed spaces contain private areas, such as the president's office and the finance department.

The logic of the geometric interior grid is counterpointed with the placement of a white spiral staircase, linking the lower floors to a resting space in the loft. When ascending these stairs the insistent logic of the form of the space could be forgotten, as the occupant falls into a light nap in their break from work.

"Inside the landscape with various levels, white boxes are put as if to make a village. There are some bypasses, hidden areas and open areas, alcoves where we can look down the atrium, also we can look over the whole area from the loft space. As if we walk inside an ancient village, we can enjoy sequential views here."

Yoshimasa Tsutsumi

2.19b

2.19b

The circular form of the spiral stair counterpoints the orthogonal geometry of its surroundings.

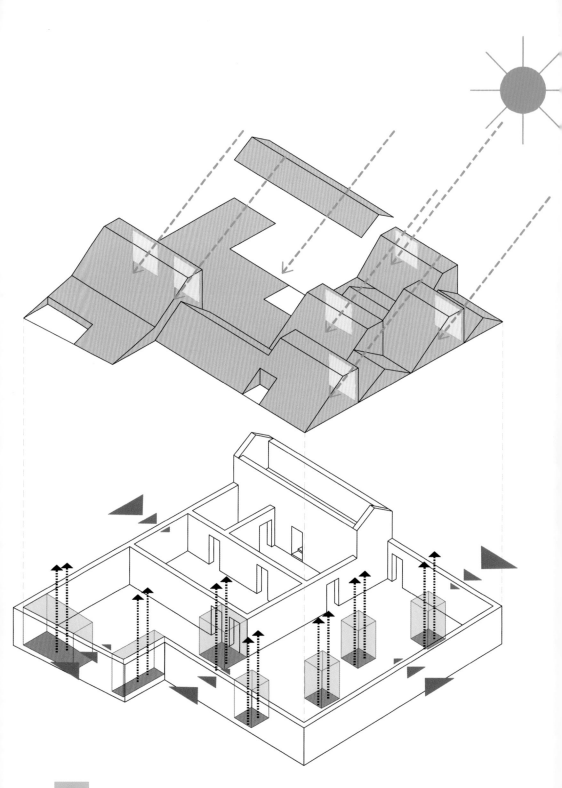

3.1

3 Sustainable Interiors

Building reuse is an extremely sustainable method of development. The reuse of an existing building to accommodate new use is a very environmentally friendly approach to the creation of new space, because the structure is already in place and quite often many of the services might already be on the site. The embodied energy in these elements can be saved through upgrade and reuse, and by adapting the existing building stock, the amount of natural resources required to construct a building is greatly reduced. As well as constructing a building or interior in a sustainable way, the designer can also create an interior that will be occupied in a sustainable manner. For example, rain and gray water can be recycled and high levels of insulation will cut the necessity for massive amounts of heating and cooling.

3.1

Name: Cooking School
Location: Cadiz, Spain
Designer: Sol 89 (María González y Juanjo López de la Cruz)

Introduction

Sustainable building reuse

It is a very environmentally friendly process to reuse existing buildings, most simply because the massive amount of energy required to build new, in terms of materials and workforce, does not have to be expended. It is of an even greater benefit if the conversion is made using sustainable techniques. The designer can select materials that do not contain huge amounts of embodied energy, that have been sourced locally and that do not harbor toxic or hazardous chemicals. Additionally, remodeling can be made more environmentally sound by considering how the building is used. It can be designed so that the minimum amount of energy is expended in the day-to-day use, and so that the environment that is created is beneficial to everyone who occupies it.

The existing building can be altered, remodeled, reclad, and refurbished. The reduction in the sheer amount of energy consumed is one of the biggest and most urgent challenges for all designers today, and so a very sensible option is to extend the lifespan of the existing building stock. Existing buildings can also be seen as an important cultural, social, and architectural resource for shaping our future. The environmental movement's international slogan: "Reduce/Reuse/Recycle" is a manifesto for the way to live in the twenty-first century, and is especially pertinent to interior architecture.

Reduce is aimed at using less, that is avoiding and minimizing waste. Reuse can apply to things of every scale, from elements of decoration and furniture to whole buildings. Recycle is an attitude to the processing of material. This means that the less the original product has to be altered, the less environmental impact in the process. The dilapidated, the strange, and the ordinary all have worth, and the designer can exploit this to create new and worthwhile architecture. It could be argued that

it is the responsibility of the designer to value what exists, to set an example and discover the potential in the already built; to develop intelligent strategies for new solutions to reuse the existing building stock.

The sustainable interior

If carbon emissions are to be addressed, then the overall lifecycle of the building needs to be confronted, not just in the construction of the building, but also in its operation including heating, cooling, and lighting. The argument for this reduction is well known: the imperative to reduce carbon emissions, combined with the imminent possibility of fuel poverty and the rising price of energy means that we must consider a more responsible future. It is well recognized that a significant proportion of the reduction can be achieved through the modification of behavior, at both the individual and the organizational level.

A change in human behavior can bring about a reduction in energy demand; the user of any building can ask themselves: "what temperature is realistically comfortable, how important is it to turn off the lights?" People can consider whether waste should be sorted into its individual components, and controversially, will the existing be adequate, is a new replacement really necessary? Attitudes that underpin these questions are bound up with collective responsibility and human rights, but the designer can help by making the questions easier to answer, with simple design decisions, such as ensuring that the interactive elements of the design are easily accessible with simple modifications available to the user. For example, by ensuring that the recycling bins are easy to access, by making certain that the cooling and heating systems are easy to operate, by having windows that open to allow fresh air into the building, and by specifying that the light switches are situated in a visible position.

Concurrently with this change in attitude towards the existing building stock, there has been the development of new intelligent concepts that link district wide, infrastructural facilities. As the primacy of the car is reduced, so the value of public transport is once again recognized, thus reducing fuel emissions, lessening the need for car parks in town centers, and encouraging people to walk more. This is combined with massive advances in digital technology, all of which have an impact upon the interior. The commuter may choose to work at home for part of the week, this will reduce the overheads for the employer and reduce the emissions connected with traveling. However, what are the consequences for the actual home in which the work is completed? Architecture and interior design could be improved to help homeworkers.

Digital technology allows homeowners to control their homes in a much more effective manner. For example, the heating can be digitally turned on at a time that is convenient for the user, rather than being set by an electronic timer; curtains can be automatically opened or closed to keep the heat in or the sun out; and lighting can be programmed to respond to the needs of the user.

One of the greatest concerns for the twenty-first-century population is the search for a sustainable future. The interior architect can help facilitate this through the creation of designs that are constructed in an environmentally friendly way and interiors that are designed to be occupied in a sustainable manner.

Retrofitting

Retrofitting is a term that is used to describe the process of refurbishing and remodeling buildings to achieve reductions in the operational energy consumption. It is an especially useful technique for saving large twentieth-century structures, particularly apartment blocks, factories, hospitals, and other municipal buildings. These structures were constructed at a time of plentiful fuel, and consequently little attention was paid to such practices as insulation and double glazing.

Sustainable Building Reuse

Passive cooling and heating

Passive cooling and heating is the practice of harnessing the natural climatic conditions to the advantage of those who occupy the building. This process includes the orientation of the interior toward natural light and ventilation. The manipulation of natural light into and through an interior can save on the use of artificial light and will also provide the occupant with a connection to the landscape outside the building. Trapped solar gain can save on heating, while natural ventilation can cool a space and minimize the need for extensive air-conditioning.

Sustainable building reuse

Name: Greenpeace Headquarters
Location: London, UK
Designer: Feilden Clegg Bradley Architects

Feilden Clegg Bradley Architects converted a 1920s factory and office building into the headquarters for Greenpeace UK in 1990. This presented a number of difficult problems for the architects. Greenpeace wanted to minimize CO_2 emissions, to remove as far as possible any factor that might contribute to "sick building syndrome" and to reduce the environmental impact of the various materials used. The project makes maximum use of the considerable window area, for the access of both natural light and ventilation. Pivoting screens fixed at the point of the external walls act in two ways to control the levels of sunlight entering the building. Firstly, as sunlight enters the building it is bounced at high level off the pivoting reflectors, across the room to reflect again from natural cotton ceiling-mounted canopies and into the center of the deep office. The pivoting screens also stop any direct penetration of natural light into the building by acting as louvers on the exterior of the building. Small casements at the top and bottom of the windows open; this encourages cross-ventilation and the movement of clean air into the depths of the building. The centrally placed open stair admits natural light into the middle of the building and aids ventilation by encouraging the stack effect. Greenpeace needed to make a statement about the environmental possibilities of reusing an existing building, Feilden Clegg Bradley fulfilled all their expectations.

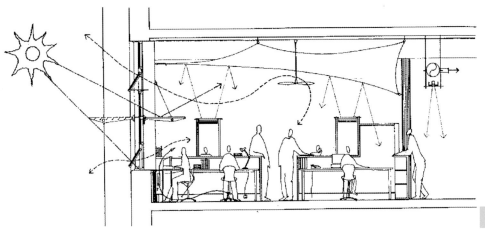

3.2a

3.2b

3.2c

3.2a

As this section drawing shows, the room is naturally lit and ventilated.

3.2b–c

The offices are constructed from carefully selected sustainable materials.

"Green design is place sensitive. One of its attractions in a globalizing world is the potential to make place-specific architecture by responding to the clues of a specific climate and site, and, where possible, using sustainable local materials."

The Energy Research Group

The Sustainable Interior

Sustainable interior architecture

Name: Edinburgh Centre for Carbon Innovation
Location: Edinburgh, UK
Designer: Malcolm Fraser Architects

The Edinburgh Centre for Carbon Innovation is a redevelopment of the eighteenth-century Royal High School. A new atrium, staircase, and social spaces have been stitched between and around the original historic building.

This central circulation route serves to tie the various new and old elements together and also provide a passive heating and cooling system. This atrium acts as a chimney encouraging air movement through the building, by pulling clean air into the building and using the stack effect, funneling upwards through the open space.

3.3a

The circulation area of the Edinburgh Centre for Carbon Innovation provides ventilation for the building. The space is lined with locally sourced timber.

3.3a

The architects have used a very limited palette of materials: sustainable cross-laminated timber, recycled copper, and locally quarried Cullalo stone. Thus the remodeled building is environmentally much more sound, the heating and cooling systems are considerably more effective, the embodied energy in the new elements is relatively small, and the occupants of the building are encouraged to be very aware of their carbon footprint in the way in which they use the buildings.

3.3b

3.3b

The interior is clad with timber panels that give it a warmth, that is in direct contrast to the severe Cullalo stone with the copper details.

3.4a

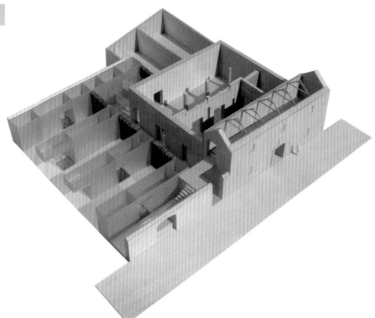

The courtyard was once used as a holding pen. It was covered over to enclose the rooms for the new cooking school.

Sustainable adaptation

Name: Cooking School
Location: Cadiz, Spain
Designer: Sol 89
(María González y Juanjo López de la Cruz)

The reuse of existing buildings, in order to accommodate new uses is a process that can be used to activate the sustainable potential of a host building. In 2007 a nineteenth-century abattoir in Medina Sidonia, near Cadiz, was adapted to house a new school of professional cooking. The existing building was organized around the gruesome process of herding, containing, and then dispatching cattle. This grisly sequence was manifested in the building by thick, high, solid walls, which hid the interior of the space; thus, the building was hidden behind a perimeter wall that contained a discrete internal courtyard.

In order to provide a sustainable space for the new school, the designers utilized distinctive elements from the regional vernacular

architecture of the building. The external courtyard was covered with a new ceramic tile roof, a local tradition necessary to reflect the harsh sun. This molded ceramic plane was punctuated by a series of folds that maneuvers light and air downwards into the internal spaces, thus ensuring a draft of cross ventilation throughout the school. The series of small patios and courtyards allow the students to grow the food and herbs that they use for cooking. The thick solid perimeter wall acts like a Trombe wall, substantial enough to keep the interior cool, whilst absorbing heat for later release. This considerably reduces the energy use of the school and helps to resist and also accommodate the unforgiving climate of the region.

3.4b

3.4b

The new ceramic roof is designed to contrast with the white render of the existing building.

3.4c

3.4c

Small interior gardens allow the students to prepare and make food with nearby plants and herbs.

"In conjunction with human needs and the factors associated with them, the understanding of environmental issues is crucial to interior designers and their practice."

Clive Edwards

4.1

4 Methods of Organizing Space

In building construction there are two predominant structure systems: load bearing and frames, as discussed in chapter 2, pages 40 and 42. These approaches lead to quite different types of spaces. Load-bearing masonry walls create small, contained rooms with openings of a limited size, while the structural frame provides the space with freedom, as the walls do not have to correspond to the position of the columns. This chapter will explore both the closed room and the free plan by examining precedents from designers who have approached the creative process using similar techniques. These methods are: symmetry, asymmetry, balance, rhythm, playstation, and addition.

4.1
Name: 192 Shoreham Street
Location: Sheffield, England
Designer: Project Orange

Introduction

Closed room

The compact and contained space created by the load-bearing system is best exemplified in the work of Adolf Loos (1870–1933). Within the design of a series of houses in Vienna, he explored the quality and ordering of three-dimensional space and its relationship with the exterior. He referred to these tight and expressive spaces as *Raumplan*.

Free plan

The open freedom of the framed structure was exploited by Le Corbusier (1887–1965), who explored the modernist possibilities of embracing new technology, liberty, and the importance of function. This was referred to as *plan libre* or free plan, which was at the heart of his "Five Points of Architecture."

4.2a

4.2a

Tristan Tzara House located in Paris, France, and designed by Adolf Loos.

4.2b

Villa Savoye located in Poissy, France, designed by Le Corbusier.

"The 5 points of a New Architecture by Le Corbusier and Pierre Jeanneret are:

    1 The Column (*les pilotis*)
    2 The Roof Garden (*les troits jardins*)
    3 The Free Plan (*le plan libre*)
    4 The Ribbon Window (*la fenêtre en longueur*)
    5 The Free Façade (*La façade libre*)

The free plan is usually taken as the focal point of these 5 points, introducing what was an essentially new architecture, one which develops from the inside towards the outside."

Arjan Hebly

Closed Room

This section will explore the concept of space as a series of closed interrelated rooms. The organization of these rooms is directly influenced by the nature of the structure of the building and the materials used in its construction.

Symmetry

Name: Villa Rotonda
Location: Vicenza, Italy
Designer: Andrea Palladio

The Villa Rotonda (1566) is a good example of a symmetrical building; not just due to the classical style of architecture, but also because of its context. The building is situated at the top of a small, gently sloping hill. The villa and the landscape are intertwined; the rise of the hill becomes the steps of the building. Because it has views in all directions, the building has four identical façades. These portico entrances lead to a circular central hall, which is highly decorated and top lit from the roof lights in the dome. The plan of the building shows four main lines of reflective symmetry, but the function has been compromised by this desire for balance and proportion. The shape and scale of the individual rooms are dictated by the harmonious arrangement of the dominant façades and round central space.

4.3a

The villa sits on the brow of the hill.

4.3b

The framed view from the entrance gate of the approach to the villa.

"The place is nicely situated and one of the loveliest and most charming that one could find; for it lies on the slopes of a hill, which is very easy to reach. The loveliest hills are arranged around it, and afford a view into an immense theatre… Because one takes pleasure in the beautiful views on all four sides, loggias were built on all four façades."

From *Palladio* by Wundram, Pape, Marton

4.3c

4.3d

4.3c

View from within the portico, out to the landscape.

4.3d

The magnificent internal rotonda.

4.3e

The plan is a tour de force of symmetry.

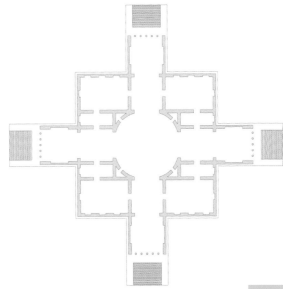

4.3e

Asymmetry

Name: Starbucks Coffee
Location: Dazaifu, Japan
Designer: Kengo Kuma Associates

Interior spaces can be designed in such a way as to defy order or balance. They can be arranged in an uneven or irregular fashion in order to promote movement or suggest fluidity in an interior. Aberration and contradiction in inside space can be manifest as distinct and innovative features, making interiors that can be memorable due to their non-conformist feel.

Two million annual visitors pass the traditional Dazaifu Tenmangu, the tenth-century shrine worshipped as "the God for Examination." In one of the low-rise buildings that line the approach to the shrine, Kengo Kuma has disrupted the orthogonal and regular shell of the building with an interior constructed from irregular timber beams.

The interior is formed from a series of woven sticks. There are 2,000 parts; all are 60 mm (2.4 inches) in section, but they vary from 1.3 meters to 4 meters (50 to 80 inches) in length. If they were stacked end-to-end they would reach as far as 4.4 kilometers (two-and-three-quarter miles). On one wall of the cave-like interior, a meandering banquette of seating is deployed. This enhances the asymmetric quality of the room. In order to invite customers into the coffee bar, a large meeting table is positioned in two halves, at the front of the shop. Its positioning, either side of the glazed front, ensures it appears to slide from outside to within, inviting customers in for a drink.

The unusual bespoke character of this well-known chain of coffee bars is an asymmetric approach to creating a unique one-off interior space.

"Dazaifu Tenmangu is a very special location, a historic shrine, for locals and visitors. I wanted to show the essence of the place to honor its strong culture of craftsmanship. If we could combine Starbucks spirit with the spirit of the artisan, we knew we could achieve something special."
Kengo Kuma

4.4a

4.4b

PLAN 1/100

4.4a

The cave-like interior is invitingly lit at night.

4.4b

An asymmetric banquette of seating zigzags through the space.

4.4c

Private and public spaces are arranged in a straightforward manner in the long thin plan.

Key:

1   ENTRANCE
2   CAFE SEATING
3   BACK BAR
4   WORK ROOM
5   MANAGER'S ROOM
6   WC
7   WC
8   MACHINE ROOM
9   GARDEN
10 AIR CONDITIONING UNIT

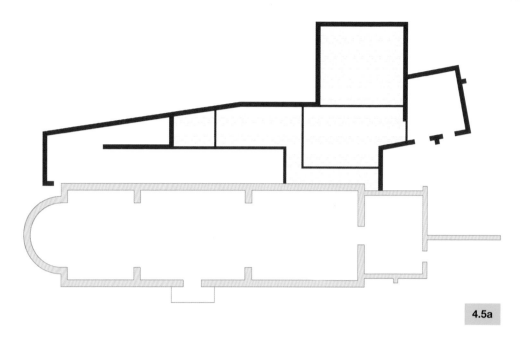

4.5a

Balance

Name: Plaster Cast Gallery, The Canova Museum
Location: Possagno, Italy
Designer: Carlo Scarpa

Interiors that are balanced do not need to be identical or even symmetrical; balance can be achieved through the careful positioning of objects, spaces, or forms.

Carlo Scarpa was asked to design the extension to the original Canova Museum to celebrate the bicentenary of the artist's birth. The gallery (or *gipsoteca*), was a large, complete, and composed classical building, Scarpa's extension (1957) is a modernist counterpoint to this monumentality. It is triangular in plan and appears to slide effortlessly through the space next to the *gipsoteca*. The initial space of Scarpa's insertion is white, top lit and more

or less cubic in shape. It has been slipped from the axis of the original foyer and thus encourages both visual and physical movement. Visitors follow their eyes around the corner and immediately appreciate the manner in which the space slides through the triangular room and into the courtyard beyond. The new and the old are separated by a lightwell that throws filtered natural light into the new gallery, reinforcing the sense of movement. The new and the old are different both in shape and in nature, but the classical and the modernist parts are similar in ambition, and strength, and are therefore balanced.

4.5b

4.5a

The drawing shows the ordered original building balanced with Scarpa's insertion.

4.5b

Light and space flows through the gallery of Segusini's original building. Scarpa mirrored the stepped ceiling and the effects of the light in his new addition.

"The architecture of Carlo Scarpa is an authentic, powerful and coherent body of work. During the course of its production he dedicated himself to a lifetime of research into the balance between form and material; craft and tradition, memory and sensuality."

George Ranalli

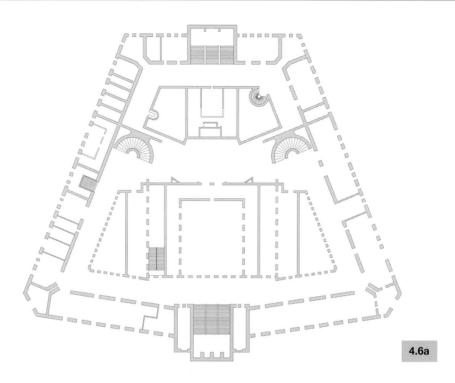

Rhythm

Name: Post Office Savings Bank
Location: Vienna, Austria
Designer: Otto Wagner

A rhythm of repeated elements can create order and control within an interior. These may be objects, structural elements, or even spaces. Elements may then be placed within the space that conform to this rhythm, or contrast with it. A dissimilar object placed within a series of similar ones will stand out, equally an element positioned at an angle will be revealed within an orthogonal organization.

The Post Office Savings Bank (1904) in Vienna is widely regarded as one of the most important examples of early modern architecture: the structure and the cladding are quite clearly expressed; the bolts that hold the marble sheets in place are openly visible. The centrally placed main banking hall is a magnificent space, with exposed columns and a curved glass roof. A strong and controlling grid dictates the position of all the major elements within the space, from the aluminum hot air blowers to the glazed panels in the floor. The pattern or rhythm of this restraining grid organizes the interior, thus liberating the in-between spaces for the post office customers.

4.6b

4.6c

4.6d

4.6e

4.6a

As this plan shows, the banking hall is placed at the heart of the post office.

4.6b

The space is ordered by the grid.

4.6c

Aluminum air vents create rhythm in the entrance hall.

4.6d

The grid is reinforced by the careful placement of the air vents.

4.6e

The glass floor emphasizes the rhythm of the grid.

"The top-lit banking hall was the closest Wagner came to his ideal of a new style derived from engineering forms. The beautifully integrated, riveted steel structure, glazing, light fittings, cylindrical heat inlets and glass block floor, and total absence of ornament make it a landmark in the development of modern architecture."

Richard Weston

Playstation

Name: Mobile Home Voor Het Kröller-Müller
Location: Kröller-Müller Museum, the Netherlands
Designer: Atelier Van Lieshout (AVL)

A particular approach that has become more prevalent within all aspects of design is similar to the organizational technique used in PlayStation or computer games. A collection of events or objects is arranged in series, each is a complete entity and has to be fully appreciated before the viewer, or competitor can move on. Just as computer-game players have to complete a particular level before they can enter the next experience. There is no interaction or movement between levels, although there is a theme that unites them. Interior designers can use this technique to create a series of different experiences or spaces.

Mobile Home by Atelier Van Lieshout is a deformed temporary structure that has been distorted to express the different activities that happen within the home. Each function is expressed as a grossly distorted protuberance that clings to the wall of the original structure. Each is recognizably complete and a total experience in its own right.

4.7a

4.7b

4.7c

4.7a

Grossly distorted protuberances spill from the caravan.

4.7b

The character of each space is expressed by its functional autonomy.

4.7c

The materials used reflect the individual function of the spaces.

"His caravans and campers do not merely express a utopian optimism, they display a desire for autonomy that is much more primitive, alluding to the vogue of survivalism, with all of its fascistic overtones. Above all, the sculptures, tools, pieces of furniture and built structures that Van Lieshout makes are direct and impulsive manifestations of a desire to create extensions of his own body."

Bart Lootsma

4.8a

4.8a

The exaggerated perspective of the fixed stage.

Addition

Name: Teatro Olimpico
Location: Vicenza, Italy
Designer: Andrea Palladio

Perfect interior spaces can be created within existing buildings to regularize an irregular space, and create order and generate formality. The designer may wish to take the approach of creating a completely new interior, which has little connection or relevance to the original space—a contained and internally focused room.

The Teatro Olimpico (1580) is based on the ancient Roman principle of a fixed and elaborate architectural backdrop or proscenium with a stage in front of it. It is a fixed and permanent autonomous element within an irregularly shaped building. This self-contained geometrical space contains the seating, the stage, and the scenery, all of which are integrated with

each other. The audience sits within the highly decorated half amphitheater, which is terminated at the top layer by a colonnade of freestanding and attached columns. Statues of the gods stand upon the columns joining the audience in their appreciation of the performance.

The stage contains a permanently fixed street scene; seven streets recede away from the viewer with exaggerated perspective. This is created by narrowing the space between the walls and gradually raising the floor. The trompe l'oeil clouds painted onto the flat ceiling reinforce this exterior quality. Palladio has created a vision of classical theater within the tight confines of a city context.

4.8b

4.8b

The view through an opening in the Proscenium Screen.

"This permanent setting, representing a city in the Renaissance style, only allowed for the performance of classical plays."

Rob Krier

Free Plan

The liberation of the internal walls from the structure allows for vast, open, free space. This section will explore the opportunities that this type of approach can offer.

Symmetry

Name: New National Gallery
Location: Berlin, Germany
Designer: Ludwig Mies van der Rohe

The structural revolution that led to the Free Plan was taken to the absolute extreme with the design of the New National Gallery, in Berlin, Germany (1968). The building was conceived as a piece of steel and glass, modernist art placed upon a plinth. The exterior walls are completely glazed, immense columns support a massive overhanging roof, the corners are free, and thus the interior space not only appears to be empty, but also recedes far beyond the limits of the building. Each elevation is treated identically, regardless of view or orientation, with just two well-proportioned black steel columns, which carry the huge flat plane of the roof. The arrangement on the interior is even more austere, although the structural grid is exposed within the ceiling, the space is free of structure and is therefore liberated. This allows the organization of the temporary exhibitions space to be completely open and unrestricted.

Ludwig Mies van der Rohe

Ludwig Mies van der Rohe is regarded as one of the pioneers of modern architecture. He developed a method of using an exposed steel structure with plate glass infills to create rigorous yet elegant spaces. Other significant buildings include the Seagram Building in New York (1958) and the German Pavilion at the Barcelona Exhibition of 1929, for which he also created the celebrated Barcelona chair. He is famous for the motto: "Less is more."

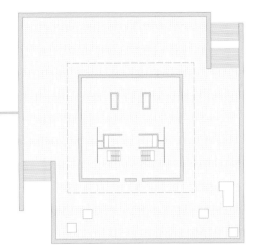

4.9a

4.9b

4.9c

4.9d

4.9a

As this plan shows, the necessary service areas are situated below ground to allow for open spaces above.

4.9b

The grid of the ceiling is visible suspended over the free space.

4.9c

The exterior clearly shows the minimal grid and free plan of the building.

4.9d

The careful placement of the columns allows clear views between them.

Asymmetry

Name: Kunsthal
Location: Rotterdam, the Netherlands
Designer: Rem Koolhaas/OMA

Spaces that have been liberated from the constraints of load-bearing walls do not have to adhere to any fixed pattern or order. The walls, spaces, and activities do not have to be placed in relation to the structure, they can be positioned in the location that is most suitable for the facilitation of the function.

The Kunsthal in Rotterdam, a museum for exhibitions and performances, is a compact building that contains a large exhibition space, distributed over three halls and two galleries.

The building is situated on top of a small road and next to a four-and-a-half-meter-high (15 feet) dyke. A series of massive ramps and roads carve through the art gallery space, creating the sense that the city is pouring through the structure. The concept is of a mobius strip-like building, a promenade that loops around and through the inclined auditorium, through a side gallery and up on to the roof. This results in a confusion or complexity to the nature and function of the spaces, an asymmetrical interior is created.

4.10a

4.10b

4.10a

The circulation flows through the lecture hall.

4.10b

The free plan allows visual links to exist through transparent walls.

4.10c

Axonometric diagram showing the architectural promenade.

4.10d

The ramps and stairs of the circulation are threaded between the columns.

4.10c

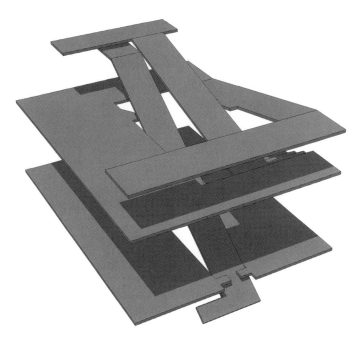

"The building was conceived as a square crossed by two routes… With these givens, and the fact that these crossings would divide the square into four parts, the challenge became: how to design a museum as four autonomous projects—a sequence of contradictory experiences which would nevertheless form a continuous spiral. In other words how to imagine a spiral in four separate squares."

Rem Koolhaas

4.10d

Balance

Name: Barcelona Pavilion
Location: Barcelona, Spain
Designer: Ludwig Mies van der Rohe

A building or space can be organized to give a sense of balance, evenness, and strength, while still possessing qualities of transience and movement.

The Barcelona Pavilion was a temporary structure, built as the German Pavilion for the 1929 International Exhibition. It was designed to project an image of an international, open, and modern German state. The building is composed of sliding vertical and horizontal planes, tied together by the tight formation of eight columns. The single-story structure has a flat plane roof supported by elegant cruciform-shaped, chrome-covered, steel columns. Two rectangular pools, one at either end, tie the building together. The smaller pool is placed centrally to the structure and is surrounded by high walls, while the larger is off-center and is free. Between these two are a series of barely defined spaces that slip into each other. Mies van der Rohe used a simple, but expensive palette of materials: marble and onyx walls, tinted reflective glass, stainless steel, and travertine. The composition is not symmetrical, but it is balanced. There is a sense of perpetual movement within the intense rhythm of spaces and planes.

"The new architecture has broken through the wall, thus destroying the separateness of inside and outside. Walls are no longer load bearing: they have been reduced to points of support. This gives rise to a new, open plan, totally different from the classical one, in that interior and exterior space interpenetrate."

Theo van Doesburg

4.11a

The planes of box-jointed marble define and organize the space.

4.11b

4.11b

View from the pool towards the main function room.

4.11c

4.11c

The roof appears to float over the minimal structure.

4.11d

Plan drawing shows the balance between the open and closed, the bright and dark spaces.

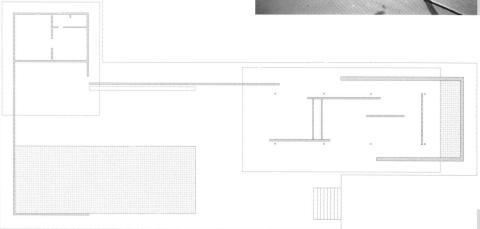

4.11d

Rhythm

Name: ALTER Concept Store
Location: Shanghai, China
Designer: 3GATTI

Whether large or small, existing or yet to be built, an interior space can possess rhythm. This spatial tempo can manifest itself in a variety of ways. Regular or irregular planning, realized through the deployment of rooms, objects, and elements, can provide a pattern or an internal logic. This can incorporate sequence, progression, and pattern. One of the roles of the designer is to orchestrate this spatial cadence.

The ALTER concept store is located in Xin Tian Di, Shanghai's busy shopping and entertainment district. Xin Tian Di is a reconstructed area of the city that replicates nineteenth-century Shanghai with a network of narrow alleys lined with Shikumen; traditional two- or three-story houses. The store is relatively small, occupying just 100 square meters of space (119 square yards), yet it needed to include a range of both public and private spaces. These included clothing display and storage, along with fitting rooms, and an office. In order to include all of these elements, the designer utilized the motif of a stair, a continuous stepped surface that could incorporate the dual function of displaying garments on its steps with the integration of more private fitting rooms and an office tucked underneath it.

The singular vocabulary of the stepped concrete ziggurat produces an interior with an unrelenting rhythmic logic; one that cascades both up and down the space. The illusion of endless space formed with the continuous stepped structure is accentuated by the placement of mannequins, perched on top of the step, both on the floor, and also attached to the ceiling. Amongst the cold concrete edges, the designer places a series of richly polished plaster plinths, upon which exquisite accessories, books, and shoes are displayed.

4.12a

4.12a

The interior "terrace" conflates floors, walls, and ceilings.

4.12b

4.12c

4.12b

Garments, objects, and the shop assistants are positioned dramatically on top of the steps.

4.12c

The sinuous organic changing rooms contrast with the hard edges of the ziggurat above it.

4.12d

The façade emphasizes the orthogonal geometrical rhythm of the interior.

4.12d

"So as a designer Francesco imagined an alternative architectural space like the ones in the drawings of Escher, where gravity and the rules of the normal world doesn't exist anymore, where there is no 'up' or 'down', no 'left' or 'right', and where everything is possible."

Giampiero Sanguigni

Playstation

Name: Dutch Pavilion, Expo 2000
Location: Hanover, Germany
Date: 2000
Designer: MVRDV

The designer can develop a concept for an interior that utilizes contrast and difference, through the creation of an installation that consists of a series of experiences that are unrelated by little more than the boundaries of the space. This is based upon the same principal as the PlayStation or computer games, where the user of the game will visit various levels of the same game, but each different stage looks and feels completely different to the last.

The Dutch Pavilion is a fine example of the playstation building; it was conceived as a reminder of land saved from the sea. It is literally six stacked floors of Dutch landscape. The visitor takes the lift to the top floor, and then gradually makes their way down, beginning with the windmills on the roof. The size of each level is the same: exactly 1,000 square meters (just over 100 square yards), but each treated differently; the fourth floor contains a forest and is supported with tree trunks. The fifth has lecture theaters and the ground floor contains a grotto. The many different aspects of Dutch life are presented together in a highly efficient, space-saving structure.

4.13a

4.13b

4.13a

The different activities on each level are clearly visible from the exterior of the building.

4.13c

The first floor is a field of flowers.

4.13b

On the third floor, enlarged structures grow up from the floor and down from the ceiling.

4.13d

Plan of the third floor.

4.13c

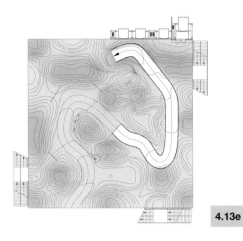

4.13e

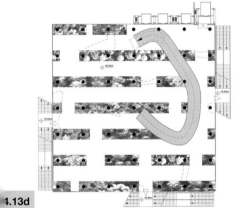

4.13d

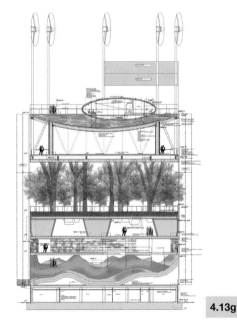

4.13g

4.13f

4.13e

Plan of the first floor.

4.13g

This section shows how each floor is occupied with a different activity.

4.13f

Plan of the ground floor.

Addition

Name: Royal Exchange Theatre
Location: Manchester, UK
Designer: Levitt Bernstein Associates

A new or alien element can be placed within a measured and balanced room or space to create an atmosphere that is no longer balanced, but one that encourages both visual and physical movement. If the object is situated off-center, if it is misaligned, then emphasis can be placed upon one space and removed from another.

The Royal Exchange Theatre in Manchester was inserted into the central hall of the old exchange building. The original space was huge and strong, with three glass domes supported by gigantic columns. The new theater really does appear as an alien element within these surroundings. It was constructed at the same time as the Pompidou Centre in Paris, and shares that optimistic, high-tech, space-age style. Massive trusses take the weight of the theater and these in turn transfer the weight onto huge columns, thus allowing the space-ship theater to float within the space. The theater is very self-contained, it is by necessity focused internally, but its placement off-center means that physical and visual movement within the hall is encouraged. The resultant larger space is used for the foyer activities, such as a café and bar, while the smaller is used primarily for circulation. It is an additive element that activates and invigorates the empty building. The empty space of the foyer is balanced by the energy of the theater.

"What is most striking about today's architecture is the impurity, the permissive joining together of the logical and the illogical, the structural and the unstructured, functional and non-functional elements."

Juhani Pallasma

4.14

The hall comfortably accommodates the theater.

4.14

5.1

5 Responsive Interiors

The existing building can be regarded as a guidebook containing much of the information necessary to provide the impetus for redesign. We can call interiors of this kind "responsive." This reading of the original space can present certain clues or pointers for the nature and character of the redesign. Not just the significant question of structural stability, but also for such issues as rhythm, movement, and space. This process can be as destructive as it is constructive. The designer or architect may strip away or remove elements in order to reveal the hidden meaning of the building, before adding elements that interpret this analysis and form the basis of the redesign. The form of the existing influences the form of the new: form follows form.

Responsive interiors can be cataloged into three sections: intervened, inserted, and installed. The architect or designer will use one of these methods to form the basis of a redesign: intervened interiors will thoroughly alter the existing building; inserted interiors will make use of the placement of an independent object, the nature of which is governed by the original building. Installed interiors will house an arrangement of a series of elements within a space that are closely related to it but will not alter it.

5.1

Name: Summer Hill Apartments
Location: Lake District, UK
Designer: Francis Roberts Architects

Introduction

Intervened interiors

Intervened interiors are created when the architect or designer reveals the qualities of the existing building and translates these into the new design. The reading of the building will lead the architect or designer to recognize the character of the original and use this as the impetus for the remodeling. This uncovering of the qualities of the original can be very intrusive and sometimes involves extensive demolition as well as construction. The interventions can alter or change the existing building so much that it can no longer viably exist independently, the new and the old can become irretrievably combined. This process is frequently exploited by the designers of museums, who strive to simultaneously exhibit both the building and its contents.

Inserted interiors

Inserted interiors establish a very close relationship between the existing building and the new interior. The architect or designer will design a single striking element to be inserted into the existing space. This distinct component may contain a number of different functional and servicing activities that can easily be separated from the main activity of the building. These could include circulation, private meeting rooms, or even huge autonomous activities such as lecture theaters. The designer may exploit the structural integrity of the existing building to support the new interior or may use the exact dimensions of a particular space to dictate the exact dimensions of the new inserted element. This technique is particularly effective when the language of the new element is at odds with the existing building: for the contemporary insertion to be dynamically juxtaposed against the crumbling ruins of the ancient building.

Installed interiors

Installed interiors allow the existing building and the elements of the redesign to exist independently. The old influences the design of the new, the arrangement and placement of the installed elements are dictated by the form of the existing, but they do not alter the structure or size of the original space—they simply react to it. Installation artists, when creating a response to a given space, will often use this technique; it is commonly employed by exhibition designers and is especially appropriate when dealing with historic or listed buildings. For example, the artist, designer, or architect may use the rhythm of the window openings or structural columns to measure the pattern of the new interior.

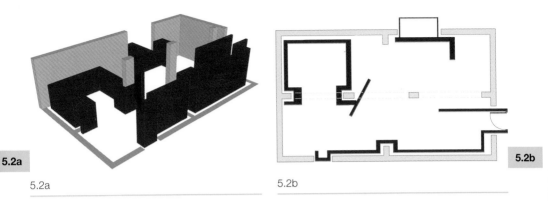

5.2a

Three-dimensional drawing of an intervened interior.

5.2b

Plan of an intervened interior.

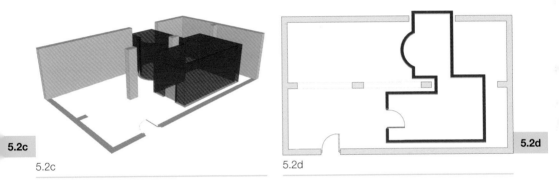

5.2c

Three-dimensional drawing of an inserted interior.

5.2d

Plan of an inserted interior.

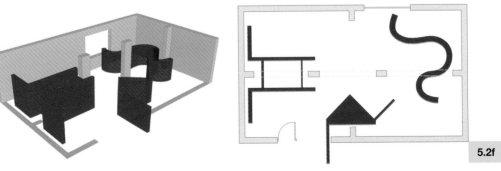

5.2e

Three-dimensional drawing of an installed interior.

5.2f

Plan of an installed interior.

Intervened

The interiors in the intervened category draw their character directly from the qualities of the existing building. An intervened interior can alter or change the existing building irrevocably so that the new and the old no longer exist independently.

Intervened: Study 1

Name: Castelvecchio Museum
Location: Verona, Italy
Designer: Carlo Scarpa

Intervention is a response that will use the qualities of the original building to inform the design of the new elements. Carlo Scarpa was the architect responsible for the restoration and remodeling of the Castelvecchio Museum (1957– 64) in Verona, Italy. By the use of creative demolition, he uncovered the various historic strata of the building. The castle was a complicated confusion of many eras of construction and Scarpa strove to explore and isolate the various phases of building to reveal the complex and rich beauty of the place.

A series of carefully designed interventions were strategically placed within the building. The dynamic quality of the modernist elements contrasted with the classical, static nature of the existing building. These elements were designed to both support and highlight the exhibits, and also to control the thresholds and movement through the building. The sparingly positioned elements encourage the visitor to move from one artefact to the next, to turn around, to move into or out of the direct light or shadow, to circulate in a composed and slightly unselfconscious manner, while appreciating the works of art, and the quality, and character of the castle.

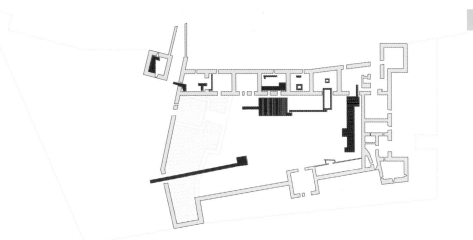

5.3a

5.3b

5.3c

5.3a

The clear and ordered organization of the original building provided a counterpoint for Scarpa's intervention.

5.3b

The pivotal point between the city walls and the castle is scraped away to reveal a backdrop for the Cangrande statue.

5.3c

The central axis links the interior spaces to the central monument of the Cangrande statue.

Intervened: Study 2

Name: Santa Monica Parking Garages
Location: California, USA
Designers: Brooks + Scarpa

An intervention-led approach to the reuse of an existing building can be utilized in order to revive and rejuvenate even the most utilitarian of structures.

Two parking garages in Santa Monica, California, had fallen into disrepair and were ruining the streetscape. With just a small budget, the designers reworked the large buildings to incorporate retail, new lighting, and a significant new street presence in order to rejuvenate what were once large and foreboding urban entities.

The designers made a series of simple interventions. These included adding a new

steel frame to the exterior of the car parks, and applying new multi-colored and textured cement board patterns, which enlivened the deadening rhythm of cars and structure. Commissioned art works completed the vibrant new façades.

The ground floor of the building was reinvigorated with retail, and each unit was enclosed with a fold-up garage door. New lighting and stairwell treatments invited car owners to return to their vehicles on foot. The future inclusion of bike stations will provide further encouragement to users to journey to the city in a healthier manner.

5.4a

5.4b

5.4a

The new car park reinvigorates the streetscape of the city.

5.4b

Artworks enliven the façade.

5.4c

Light installations have transformed what was once a foreboding space.

5.4c

Intervened: Study 3

Name: Fourth Church of Christ Scientist
Location: Manchester, UK
Designer: OMI Architects

The complex process of adapting buildings for new uses can sometimes contain a destructive element. The building may have to undergo extensive demolition before the constructive process of remodeling can begin. OMI used this approach when they carved a chapel from the innermost spaces of a disused office block. Their careful analysis focused primarily inwards, upon the quality of the individual spaces, the relationship between one room and another, and of each floor with the one below or above. The positions of the doors, the windows, and the circulation areas all contributed to this intricate composition.

The chapel itself is an atmospheric triple-height space cocooned within the depths of the building. It is subtly lit from large, west-facing windows and the long, evening sun glows through the circulation areas to provide the congregation with secondary yet evocative light. This is reinforced by artificial light secreted behind structural openings, and thus the chapel is radiant with hidden luminosity. A tiny reading room was inserted into the barely double-height space of the reception area and bookshop. This clever little structure contains bookshelves and a service desk at the lower level and a quiet retreat above.

The reading of the interior spaces of the original building provided the catalyst for the organization of the remodeling. The whole structure is a carefully composed series of delicate and subtle details, each exposing the qualities of the existing context while also enhancing the new function.

5.5a

The circulation insulates the chapel from the outside world.

5.5b

The triple height chapel is illuminated by concealed lighting.

5.5c

As this section shows, the compact interior is a collection of intricate spaces.

Inserted

The interiors in the inserted category establish a very close relationship between the existing building and the new interior. The new element is built to an exact fit of the existing building.

Inserted: Study 1

Name: Documentation Center for the Third Reich, Nazi Party Rally Grounds
Location: Nuremberg, Germany
Designer: Günther Domenig

A contemporary insertion can act as a symbolic and forceful statement. The Kongresshalle in Nuremberg was the centerpiece of the "City of Congress"; it was planned by Albert Speer to host the great Nazi rallies of the 1930s. The huge building was vacant from 1945, mainly because nobody knew what to do with it, and equally, nobody wanted to simply raze it.

The architect Günther Domenig won the competition to remodel the great building in 1998. The approach he took was to diagonally pierce the structure, directly against the grain of the building, with an uncompromising and dynamic element. This aggressively sharp shaft of glass and steel serves as a circulation route through the building, linking the entrance with the massive courtyard at the back of the building. The brutality with which it cuts the existing spaces is left exposed; the raw and scarred walls are not repaired. The insertion is an unambiguous and powerful statement of repentance and remembering.

5.6a

5.6a

Diagonal cross section through the courtyard block.

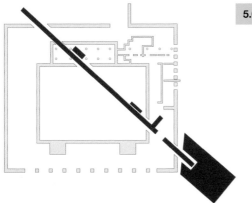

5.6b

5.6c

5.6d

5.6b

The plan shows exactly how violent the insertion is.

5.6c

The shard of circulation explodes from the building.

5.6d

The entrance is placed on a diagonal axis through the Kongresshalle.

Inserted: Study 2

Name: The Archbishopric Museum
Location: Hamar, Norway
Designer: Sverre Fehn

An insertion does not need to be an efficient, compact structure; it can be a free-ranging and abundant construction. In his remodeling of the Archbishopric Museum (1967–79) Sverre Fehn created an awkward, loose circulation route threading through the ruins of a medieval fortress that explains and reveals the history and beauty of the place it navigates.

The museum is a collection of long thin buildings gathered around an open courtyard, and the new path is a huge fluctuating structure that controls the route taken by the visitor, while also revealing the quality of the ancient building. This brutal concrete element begins as a ramp in the courtyard and then swings away from the building before performing a u-turn and diving

through an opening at the junction between the south and central wings. Once inside, it acts as a bridge, navigating the route through what were once the main rooms of the settlement. Huge floating boxes of shuttered concrete are attached to the bridge and these hold the precious archaeological discoveries belonging to the museum.

The language of this insertion is uncompromising, but it is balanced by the equally hard nature of the original building; unfinished concrete against stone and rubble. The walkway slides exactly through the existing openings and takes advantage of the light from the original windows and doors.

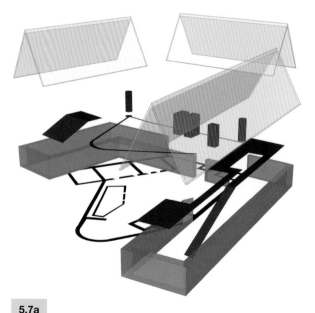

5.7a

5.7a

The awkward circulation route threads through the enigmatic buildings.

5.7b

The uncompromisingly brutal ramp begins its journey in the courtyard.

5.7c

The imposing shuttered concrete box is attached to the bridge and holds the precious archaeological finds.

5.7d

The walkway is suspended above the archaeological remains in the main hall.

5.7b

5.7c

5.7d

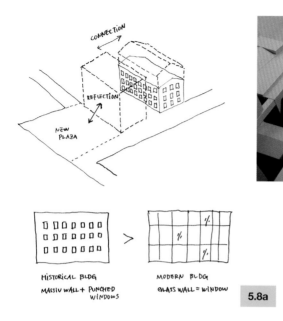

5.8b

HISTORICAL BLDG
MASSIV WALL + PUNCHED
WINDOWS

MODERN BLDG
GLASS WALL = WINDOW

5.8a

Inserted: Study 3

Name: Rotermann's Old and New Flour Storage
Location: Tallinn, Estonia
Designer: Hanno Grossschmidt, Tomomi Hayashi,
Yoko Azukawa/HGA (Hayashi–Grossschmidt Arhitektuur)

An inserted project is often realized through the placement of a new element upon, around, alongside, underneath, or on top of an existing building. This approach to reusing what already exists can create an intense dialogue, and ultimately a concentrated discourse between the old and the new interior and building.

Located between Tallinn's old town and the city port is the Rotermann Quarter, a former industrial area notable primarily for food production and storage. The 1904 flour storage warehouse was designated as the centerpiece of a new regeneration plan. This included a new public square and an additional building that contained retail space on the ground floor and office space on the upper floor.

A new building was designed adjacent to the warehouse and a glazed connection linked the two spaces. The façades of the new block were designed as scaled, proportional, abstracted versions of the industrial warehouses. In order to relate and to strengthen the character and dialogue between the new and the already existing buildings, the new insertions were designed in a robust manner. The inserted two-story addition, along with the new block, were both clad in Corten steel. This complemented and at the same time was in deference to the raw concrete frame, the rough limestone surfaces, and the brick lintels of the industrial architecture.

5.8c

5.8d

5.8e

5.8a and 5.8b

The sketch and the model clearly demonstrate the relationship between the new, the old buildings, and the public square.

5.8c

Circulation is used to link the new building with the existing warehouse.

5.8d

The existing masonry structure contrasts with the new Corten steel clad insertions.

5.8e

One of the office spaces.

Installed

The interiors in the installed category allow the existing building and the new elements of the design to exist independently of one another.

Installed: Study 1

Name: Captain Melville Restaurant
Location: Melbourne, Australia
Designer: Breathe Architecture

The reuse of historic buildings will often involve the careful consideration and assessment of the existing architecture. This is in order to establish if it is of significant historical or cultural value and therefore will need to be conserved. The designers may react to this test by placing a series of elements into the interior that do not alter or even touch the building in a structural manner, but which may completely transform the atmosphere of the space.

Mac's Hotel, constructed in 1853 in the center of Melbourne, was one of the first licensed premises in the city. Now listed on the Victorian Heritage Register, the hotel was built in the middle of the Australian gold rush of the 1850s. Melbourne had then grown almost overnight from a tiny village into a huge tent city, an immense grid of temporary shelters, packed full of prospectors all seeking their fortune.

The image of a solid structure once surrounded by a never-ending sea of canvas forms influenced the designer's reuse of the historic building. The designers have allowed the interior to become "colonized" by a series of simple peaked forms, erected from basic materials such as steel, timber, leather, and canvas.

Divided into two main parts, the front part of the building contains a central bar with tables and chairs lining the perimeter. The back part contains a large dining hall and services such as the kitchen and bathrooms. The prospector's metaphor is realized through the deployment of a series of framed tent-like structures arranged over the long dining tables. Reminiscent of the tents that once contained prospectors searching for gold, the symbolic temporary enclosures now contain people looking forward to the prospect of their dinner.

5.9a

5.9d

5.9b

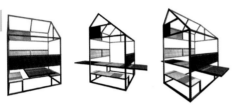

5.9c

5.9a

The prominently positioned bar greets patrons as they enter the space.

5.9b

These axonometric drawings show the steel-framed tent structures.

5.9c

In order to evoke the history of the city, tent-like structures are placed over the dining tables.

5.9d

Once surrounded by tents, the hotel is now encircled by high-rise towers.

Installed: Study 2

Name: Pheasant Barn
Location: Faversham, UK
Designer: Circus Architects

An installed interior will acknowledge the qualities of the existing building without actually altering them. This approach is especially suitable for work within listed buildings as substantial or irreversible changes to the building are unlikely to be permitted.

This was the problem that Circus Architects faced when they were asked to convert a Grade II listed, seventeenth-century barn into a family home. They were unable to change the exterior of the building or touch four large, exposed timber trusses that supported the wooden weather-boarded barn. This led the architects to

design elements that just slipped between the existing structure, allowing the new, and the old to exist simultaneously without intruding upon each other.

The four trusses effectively divided the interior into five sections. Accordingly, within this rhythm, two floating balconies were installed, leaving the ground floor area free for family activities, while providing bedroom privacy in the floating structures. The undersides of the mezzanines also provided some order to the lower level by dictating the position of particular activities.

5.10a

5.10a

The language of the new and old is radically different.

5.10b

View through the barn interior, towards the floating bedroom.

5.10c

In this axonometric drawing, the rhythm of the existing counterpoints the disorder of the installation.

5.10d

As this section shows, the ordered timber structure contrasts with the new, dynamic, pure white elements.

"The combination of old structures and new uses calls for specific solutions depending upon the relevant object and task… the genius loci is reinvigorated through conversion."

Johan Jessen and
Jochem Schneider

5.10b

5.10c

5.10d

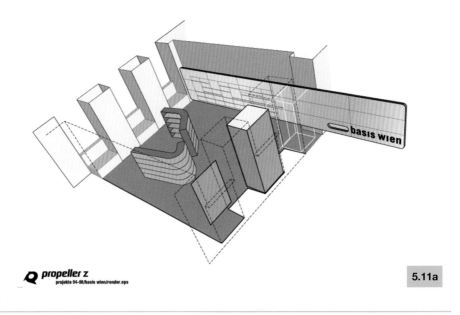

propeller z
projekte 94-98/basis wien/render.eps

5.11a

5.11a

As this axonometric diagram of the project shows, the screen is part of a family of installed elements.

Installed: Study 3

Name: Basis Wien, Information Center for Contemporary Art
Location: Vienna, Austria
Designer: propeller z

An installed object can evoke feelings of lightness and movement when placed within a calm and measured space. Designers, propeller z, juxtaposed a long interactive screen against the calm interior of a single room in their remodeling of an eighteenth-century block in the museum quarter of Vienna.

This elongated element is lit from behind and below, and appears to float. The function of the long silver plane changes as it travels through the coffered room. It is used for the storage of archive material, for small exhibition displays and to accommodate computer and other communication equipment within the public area. It then glides out through a new transparent glass door set into the Baroque façade and signals the entrance to the center with a simple yellow logo.

The screen is constructed in a most simple manner; cut sheets of aluminum are attached to a straightforward steel frame using kitchen cabinet fittings. The lack of polish within the construction is balanced by the decaying qualities of the original room. The impact of this long aluminum element is huge, but the damage to the original vaulted space is minimal.

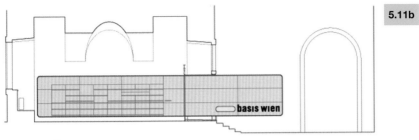

5.11b

5.11c

basis wien

5.11d

propeller z

Designers, propeller z, have developed a game, "super trumpf" (not unlike Top Trumps) involving the work of their practice. It has categories such as floor area, construction time, and budget. The exhibition building, Meteorit, had the longest thinking time at 11,532 hours, while the portable sound reproduction unit, Spin Off, had the shortest at just 13 hours.

5.11b

The screen is an independent element that links the outside with the inside.

5.11c

The backlit screen appears to float within the interior space.

5.11d

The screen slides through the entrance to advertise the information center.

6.1

6 Autonomous Interiors

The shaping or organization of interior space can sometimes be regarded as an independent process, constrained only by the extent of the established spatial volume. The original building can be thought of as an envelope that contains the new interior while exerting very little influence upon it. The new elements are positioned within the space, referring only to themselves, not to the container that they are placed within. This approach can be used to standardize unusual spaces or structural systems, thus creating what appears to be a composed and ordered space from what is actually irregular and unbalanced.

Considerations such as function, style, fashion, surface treatment, and contemporary art and design can be discussed through the arrangement and juxtaposition of form and lighting.

Autonomous interiors can be cataloged into three sections: disguised, assembled, and combined. The architect or designer will use the disguised approach to line or hide the existing space; the assembled system to fill the space with new objects, and when these two are used simultaneously, the method can be described as combined.

6.1

Name: MAXXI Museum
Location: Rome, Italy
Designer: Zaha Hadid Architects

Introduction

Disguised interiors

Disguised interiors treat the existing interior as a shell that is to be hidden or camouflaged. The architect or designer will create a new lining to cover the surfaces of the original space. This will, in effect, give the appearance of a completely new interior. It can provide an irregular space with balance and a sense of proportion that it would not naturally have. This lining or veil has qualities that are independent of the original building; its material, structural and physical characteristics are very much self-governing; dictated by function, style, or whim. It is constrained only by the size of the space that it inhabits. The lining will usually barely touch the building's walls at all. This screen can be used to conceal unsightly or intrusive elements; service activities such as circulation or bathrooms can be secreted behind it, and it can even fold to hide away whole rooms. This approach is typically used within retail design.

Assembled interiors

Assembled interiors are generally anonymous spaces that do little more than contain a series of usually interconnected objects. The space itself is typically undistinguished and is, as a rule, treated in a neutral manner. The idea is for attention to be drawn away from the qualities of the building and for the focus to be upon the elements displayed within the space. This is typically the approach that an exhibition designer would take: the collection of exhibits, all of which relate to each other, are displayed in a fairly indistinct room. The objects interact with each other, the rhythm and placement of each is carefully planned with great consideration for those other related exhibits, and as such, the installation is designed to be independent from the form and structure of the existing space.

Combined interiors

Combined interiors bring together the disguised and assembled approaches. The existing space is regarded as a neutral box that is lined or hidden. This newly formed space is then inhabited by a series or collection of elements, all interacting with each other and with the lining or screen, but not with the original space or building. The only constraint is size, which dictates exactly how much of this particular design concept can fit into the space. This approach is typical of most mainstream retail design. The designer will develop a concept that is transferable—nationally or even internationally. The shop walls are lined with display units, while the interior space contains freestanding cabinets or counters. The style will distinguish a particular brand and the design has to be sufficiently flexible to allow it to adapt to many different spaces and locations.

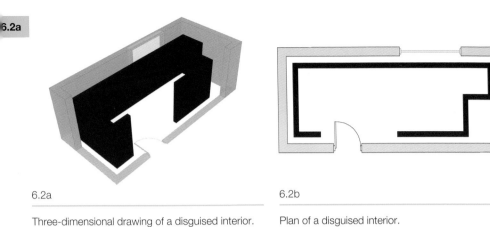

6.2a

Three-dimensional drawing of a disguised interior.

6.2b

Plan of a disguised interior.

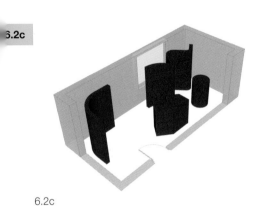

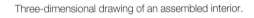

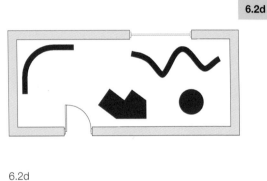

6.2c

Three-dimensional drawing of an assembled interior.

6.2d

Plan of an assembled interior.

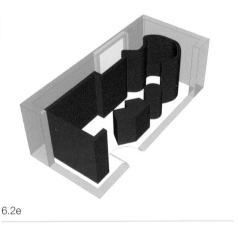

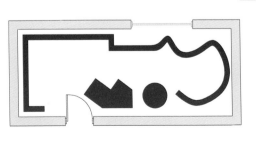

6.2e

Three-dimensional drawing of a combined interior.

6.2f

Plan of a combined interior.

Disguised

The interiors in this category treat the existing as a shell that is to be hidden or camouflaged. The interior will often consist of a new lining that disguises the surface of the existing space.

Disguised: Study 1

Title: Oki-ni
Location: London, UK
Designer: 6a Architects

An uneven or crooked interior can be provided with order by the insertion of a facing or lining. This new element will have its own organization and geometry and will inflict this discipline upon the existing space. Oki-ni, which means "thank you" in the Osaka dialect, occupies what used to be two adjoining retail spaces. This interior space was both irregular and slightly unknown, because the architects were unable to survey the building before work commenced on site. 6a proposed a horizontal "tray" that could be slid into the space, unifying both halves and absorbing the central structural column, which had been hidden in the separating partition wall. The tray was able to accommodate any irregularities in the outline of the space and thus created a meaningful order to the retail space. The structure of Russian oak controls and delineates the floor area, and the upturn at the edges exhibits and displays the range of clothing and accessories. Clothes are hung from the exaggerated skirting and are also draped over the large felt stacks in the center of the space. The interstitial spaces behind the walls contain the subsidiary services such as storage, changing rooms, and staff areas. The simple new element houses all of the shop's functional requirements while also inflicting rigor upon an uneven and unfortunate space.

6.3a

The Russian oak "tray" controls and disguises the space.

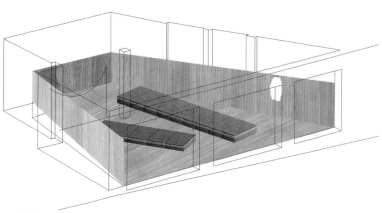

6.3a

6.3b

The plan view shows the difference
between the new and the old.

6.3c

A simple model shows the designer's
strategy of a new regular lining
placed within an irregular space.

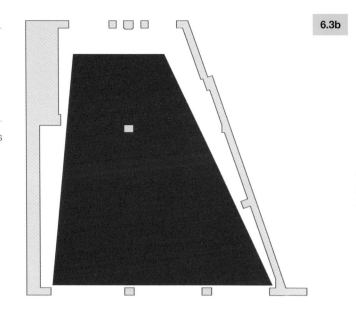

6.3b

6.3c

6.3d

6.3e

6.3d

The stack of felt sits enigmatically in the space.

6.3e

The exaggerated skirting does not reach the ceiling
of the space.

Disguised: Study 2

Name: American Bar/Kärntner Bar
Location: Vienna, Austria
Designer: Adolf Loos

An interior can be created to clad the existing interior envelope of the space it is to inhabit. It will completely cover the internal walls, floor, and ceiling. Adolf Loos explored the principles of cladding, whether of the interior or the exterior. He regarded covering as the oldest architectural detail, and that this mask should be truthful to the materials used.

The Kärntner or American Bar (1907) uses skillful manipulation of a small space in Vienna. It is situated on a quiet side street, Kärntner Durchgang and the outside signage is a representation of the American flag in gaudy-colored glass, a provocative gesture in the city where Loos was renowned for his caustic character and controversial newspaper column, *Das Andere*.

The inside is significantly different to the exterior: a skillful composition of marble, onyx, mirror, and timber lines the space to form a discrete, intimate interior. The space is given careful order through the organization of Skyros marble pillars and beams, reinforced by a veined marble coffered ceiling and then exaggerated by mirrors on the end walls, in effect "multiplying the image to infinity."[1] This creates endless rooms beyond the solidity of the timber lining and exaggerates the theatricality of the tiny room. The mahogany and leather furniture and brass counter are organized around the edges of the room, thus leaving the axial center of the space for circulation. The modest space seats only twenty or so, and yet is not claustrophobic, thus ensuring an interior of both order and intimacy.

[1] Gravagnuolo, B. and Rossi, A. 1982 *Adolf Loos*. New York: Edizioni.

6.4a

6.4b

6.4a

Upper level mirrors inside the bar exaggerate what is actually a very intimate space.

6.4b

A vivid representation of the American flag advertises the bar.

6.4c

The plan reveals the incredibly tight organization of the interior.

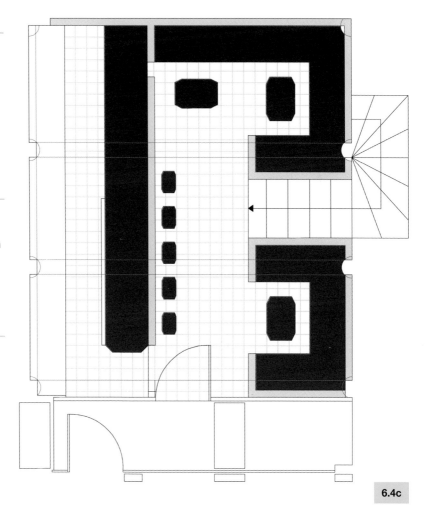

6.4c

Raumplan

Adolf Loos (1870–1930) developed the notion of *Raumplan* or space plan, an intricate three-dimensional organization of space. This is most perfectly realized in three houses: the Moller House, the Müller House, and the Tristan Tzara House.

6.5a

The drama of the two parasitical "disruptions" in the space is emphasized in a concept sketch of the project.

Disguised: Study 3

Name: Studio Pastrengo
Location: Milan, Italy
Designer: Atelier Forte

Autonomous interiors can give harmony to a disordered space or they can disrupt the balance in an already well-ordered room. The design of an autonomous disguised interior can sometimes be generated through the development of a narrative, a story that may emerge from a sketch or a painting and which can be utilized in order to disguise or camouflage the space in which it is placed.

In a large double-height room in a warehouse in Milan, Atelier Forte disrupted the interior of the space by creating two new rooms to house private meeting spaces. They created two new mezzanine levels in the room, both of which emerge from opposite ends of the space. Akin to two "disruptions" in the lining of the space, each room appears to grow from the surface of the space. Like parasites, both in direct confrontation with each other, the rough and ready assembly of the rooms suggests a thrown together aesthetic. One that appears contingent whilst adding to the disruptive nature of the interior.

6.5b

Each element is fabricated from off-the-peg timber sections.

6.5c

The dramatic installation is intended to disrupt the space and disturb the visitor.

Assembled

The interiors in this category are defined by the character of the newly designed elements, rather than the neutral container in which they are placed. Their arrangement is designed to be independent from the form and structure of the existing space.

Assembled: Study 1

Name: MAXXI Museum
Location: Rome, Italy
Designer: Zaha Hadid Architects

Zaha Hadid Architects have, over many years, developed a style of architecture that emphasizes fluid movement and flexible use. This is exactly the approach that they have taken for the MAXXI Museum in Rome. The continuity of the interior and the lack of internal divisions allow for the display of any type of exhibition, and the dynamic and interactive spaces mean that multiple activities can simultaneously occur.

The architects describe the museum not as an enclosure but rather as a campus for art. The ambiguity that exists within the building means that the internal elements can be placed and replaced as and when necessary; the interior is permanently in a state of flux looking for the next opportunity for transformation. The limited palette accentuates the dynamic form of the museum, and the sheer massiveness, the almost urban scale of the interior, means that the interior spaces almost become public squares in which small building-sized pieces of furniture are carefully placed.

Transferability

The concept for a particular assembled interior can be transferred to anywhere in the world, because there is little relationship between the building and the new interior, it is really only a matter of how much of the design can be used at each location.

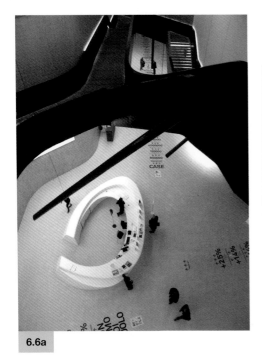

6.6a

6.6b

6.6a

The foyer space is a large, somewhat ambivalent space, deliberately so it can accommodate different activities of various sizes.

6.6b

Natural light is supplemented by artificial illumination to highlight the organic circulation areas.

"In all its roles, the street is the link between the public and the private, at scales that range from the sidewalk access of a row house to movement networks that serve major facilities. And this applies to interior streets too."

Denise Scott Brown in *AA Files 56*. AA Publications 2010

Assembled: Study 2

Name: Fendi Showroom
Location: Paris, France
Designer: Lazzarini Pickering Studio

Lazzarini Pickering devised a geometric language for the 2002 flagship Fendi showroom in Paris. The concept, which characterizes the opulent luxurious brand, was internationally transferable. The image was opulent, dynamic and generous; long sculptural elements of architectural proportions interacted three-dimensionally with each other. The units towards the center climbed to form a three-dimensional sculptural staircase, emphasizing the upper floors, while others slid delicately through the shop, exaggerating the length and space, thus ensuring that the entire shop was on view. The units that touched the edges of the space (that is the floors and the walls) were of dark wood, those in the middle of raw waxed steel. The orthogonal order of these display fittings allowed the clothes to be placed informally, almost carelessly, encouraging the customers to linger and touch. Rearranging the seasonal exhibits was a simple and straightforward task in the minimal interior. Fashion is an art that continually needs to be updated and restyled, and so this dynamic and interesting interior has already been replaced with a new design which is much more open and sober.

The collection of simple basic forms, of strong dark elements against plain, white-painted walls created a dramatic interior of light and shade.

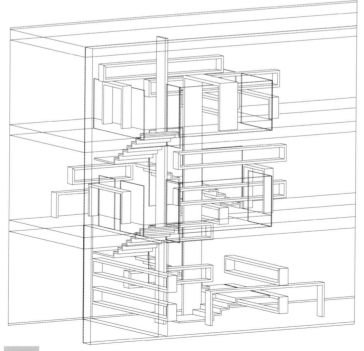

6.7a

6.7a

Display units organize and accentuate the volume of the interior.

6.7b

Accessories are placed almost carelessly upon the sliding planes.

6.7c

The dynamic quality of the furniture creates an illusion of three-dimensional movement.

6.7b

6.7c

Assembled: Study 3

Name: "Para-site" exhibition
Location: New York, USA
Designer: Diller Scofidio + Renfro

An assembled installation can inhabit apparently arbitrary places within an interior, without altering the building, or being altered by it. The radical design practice, Diller Scofidio + Renfro created such an installation at the Museum of Modern Art in New York in 1989. The exhibition questioned the premise upon which people visit a museum. Was it to view the exhibits or was it to be seen within the confines of a museum?

The installation observed and recorded the visitors' reactions to the museum. Video cameras were positioned above the revolving entrance door of the museum, other CCTV cameras monitored the escalators, while cameras attached to convex security mirrors were placed within the sculpture court, all to capture images of the museum visitors. These

images were then relayed to a series of monitors within the gallery spaces. Although the TV screens were fairly standard, the structure that supported them was an extended construction made of individual elements with exposed fixings and trailing wires. The escalators, revolving doors, corridors, and shop spaces are also the standard elements of shopping malls and convenience stores and, as such, they are the elements that inhabit the spaces of commerce and consumption. The live feeds from the elevators, escalators, thresholds, and courtyard relayed images of the approaching visitors to the viewers in the gallery, thus blurring the distinction between the subject and the object; the viewer and the viewed.

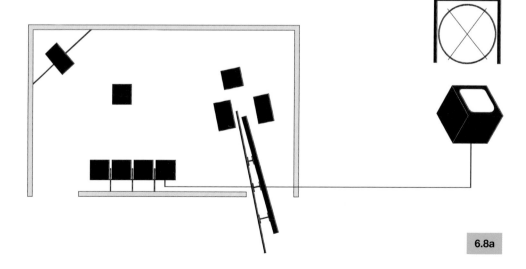

6.8a

6.8b

6.8a

The installation is an assembled collection of standard parts.

6.8b

The invasive quality of the installation dominates the white space of the gallery.

6.8c

An unsuspecting museum visitor becomes the subject of the exhibition.

6.8d

Standard TV monitors contrast strongly with the bespoke structural supports.

6.8c

6.8d

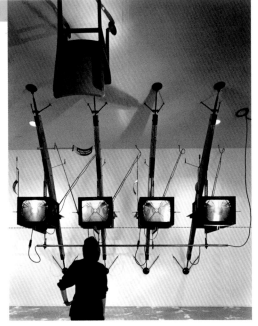

Combined

The interiors in the combined category utilize both the assembled and disguised approaches to organizing interior space. The existing space is regarded as a neutral box that is lined and then inhabited by a series of elements.

Combined: Study 1

Name: Restaurant Georges, Pompidou Centre
Location: Paris, France
Designer: Jakob + Macfarlane

An autonomous design can be considered to be freestanding with little or no connection to the site in which it is placed. Both the disguised and the assembled strategies have been used in this project. Restaurant Georges occupies the sixth floor of the Pompidou Centre, the groundbreaking arts center designed by Rogers and Piano in 1977. The elements of the interior not only could not touch the listed HVAC fittings, but it also had to be incredibly lightweight to avoid any heavy loading on the thin slab floors. The design of the restaurant is based on a tacit acknowledgement of the dominating structural grid, yet the designers imploded the constraining frame and, through digital manipulation, created a design whereby a series of outrageously swollen globular forms house the various activities of the restaurant.

The new oversized brushed aluminum shapes burst out of the floor grid to become organic bulbous containers for different functions: the bar, private dining space, reception, kitchen, and toilets. The interiors of these are coated with colored rubber: yellow for dining, red for bar, gray for the kitchen, and green for reception and toilets.

A floor of matching aluminum was laid over the existing floor, and it is this skin that is distorted, thus creating a new interior that disregards the unrelenting intellectual logic of the original building, but explodes in colorful anarchy.

Concrete

Concrete is formed from a mixture of cement, water, and an aggregate (usually stone, or gravel or a fine sand). It is extremely strong when in compression and in tension when enhanced with steel reinforcement bars. Through casting, it can be formed into many different shapes and forms and it can have a variety of textures, colors, and finishes.

6.9a

The yellow rubber lining of the private dining space has an intimate glow.

6.9b

Swollen globular pods contrast with the orthogonal organization of the Pompidou Centre.

6.9b

6.9c

The dining space is organized according to the 800 mm (31.5 inches) grid of the rest of the building—even the chairs are 800 mm (31.5 inches) wide.

6.9c

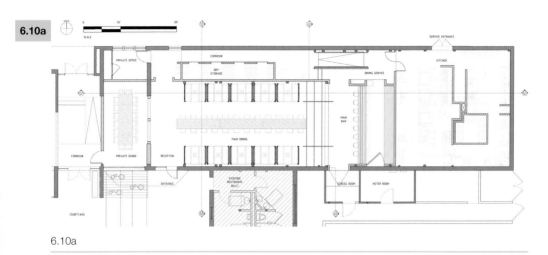

6.10a

As this plan of the space shows, a centrally placed monolithic table links the main bar with the entrance.

Combined: Study 2

Name: WORKSHOP
Location: California, USA
Designer: SOMA

An existing building will exercise little or no influence on the design of an autonomous interior. Only the volumetric constraints of the host building will influence the manner in which the interior is designed. It will do this by providing the parameters of the established spatial volume that has been designated to host the new space. The rest of the design and construction processes will regard the arrangement of space, furniture, and light into a harmonious whole.

The interior of the WORKSHOP restaurant has been designed to be in complete contrast to the 1926 Spanish Colonial style shed in which it is housed. The remodeled interior (2012) has been designed to resemble a monolithic concrete

basilica. The long rectangular shed contains a restaurant and bar for ninety-eight covers to eat, drink, and socialize in a variety of settings.

The public spaces of the shed are arranged into three zones. Adjacent to the entrance is a large dining table. At the opposite end of the shed is the main bar. In between these two spaces is the main dining room lined with two parallel banks of perimeter "booths"; smaller spaces for more intimate dining. A monolithic slab of an 11-meter-long concrete communal table links and dominates the center of the space. It intensifies the stark contrast between the vernacular exterior and the cool crisp church-like interior.

6.10b

The horizontality of the bar is emphasized by lighting at ground level and just below the counter, thus visually emphasizing the length of this important element.

6.10c

6.10c

Intimate dining booths line the main space containing the communal table.

6.10d

Leather upholstery and soft, cubed seating is used to contrast with the cold, hard concrete furniture.

6.10d

6.11a

As this diagram shows, colored lines organize and control the interior.

Combined: Study 3

Name: APOC for Issey Miyake
Location: Paris, France
Designer: Bouroullec Brothers

Function can often be the generating factor for the design of an interior; it can be substantially more influential than the quality of the space itself. The objects that are to be used within the space will often influence the creation of an autonomous interior.

The new elements of an interior can be insubstantial, quite slight, thin, and fairly lightweight, and yet so vivid that they dominate the space that they inhabit. This was the approach taken by Bouroullec Brothers when they designed the APOC store for Issey Miyake in 2000. The interior of the shop was clad with lines of clean white and brightly colored Corian (a solid moldable plastic). Just three colorful horizontal lines form the space: they circumnavigate the room, attached to, but proud of the plain white painted walls. They define and give character to the otherwise anonymous shop. Bright folded units, also cut from the same plastic material,

populate the interior. They stretch and extend into the shop, hovering graciously in the center, to act as a cutting table, an ironing board, or simply to display the clothes.

The concept came directly from a process of producing continuous tubes of fabric developed by Miyake. A computer will program an industrial knitting or weaving machine with the customer's requirements, and this creates the clothing from a single unbroken thread. A truly industrial process, the thread goes in at one end and the finished article of clothing emerges from the other. The customer is encouraged to participate in the design process, so the interior acts as a studio, factory, and shop. The new elements define the shape and character of the unspecific area; it is a process that can be adapted for practically any interior. The design was generated by the nature of the products on sale and the process used to construct them.

6.11b

6.11c

6.11d

6.11b

Garments are quite casually displayed in the space.

6.11c

The lines of Corian disguise the form of the original building.

6.11d

These organizing elements also display the clothes.

6.11e

Central display units slide through the space.

6.11e

7.1

7 Elements for Organizing Space

The strategy for organizing space will inform the plan or layout of a building, but it is the elements within the space that actually give it personality: what it feels like, how it sounds, and what it looks like. The elements are the individual components of the building, the separate details. They are an expression of the use and of the character of a building. It is these elements that distinguish or make different one place from another. The elements give character; they define the quality, and provide the features of a building, and it is the tactical deployment of them that gives the remodeled building or space its individual nature. The whole building can be understood through the reading of the details. For example, the design of a strategically placed element, such as a wall or a staircase can be very different depending upon the circumstance. Its position, the materials that it is constructed from, its individual purpose, and the pursuit of the designer will all contribute to the design. It is the relationship between these individual and specific elements that will impart atmosphere, personality, and disposition.

7.1

Name: The Jane Restaurant
Location: Antwerp, Belgium
Designer: Piet Boon® Studio

Introduction

Object

An object or series of objects can provide focus to a space, facilitate or encourage movement, supply rhythm or balance and promote direction, both visual and physical. They can be at the scale of an objet d'art or piece of furniture, or they can possibly be much larger constructions, such as pods or pavilions.

Plane

Planes are normally vertical or horizontal, mostly taking the form of walls and floors or ceilings. They define and organize in that they control the visual and physical limits of a space. However, they can be so much more than a pure surface; walls can act as containers, they can hide or disguise things, ceilings can create atmosphere or indicate route, and floors can give clarity and direction.

Sequence

Sequence is generally referred to as circulation; it is usually either vertical or horizontal, and takes the form of stairs, lifts, or paths, or corridors. These areas of circulation are often the only public spaces in a building and as such, can serve to bind the disparate activities together.

Light

Light will reveal space and define form. Whether natural or artificial, it can accentuate objects or spaces, suggest direction and aid the understanding of a building. Light is an essential element and the skillful articulation of it can influence the experience of a building.

Threshold

Thresholds establish physical and visual relationships between objects and places. They can indicate the next part of the journey or become a reminder of things already experienced. They can be highly decorated and reveal the end of one encounter and the beginning of the next, or they can be so modest that they do not interfere with the experience of the journey at all.

Texture

The texture of an element describes the very materials that it is made from. It is the stuff that is touched, felt, or handled. The specific choice of materials imparts character; this surface establishes a direct relationship between human contact and the building. It not only has to provide ergonomic and environmental strength when necessary, but also has to signal personality.

7.2a

7.2b

7.2c

7.2a

Chapel of Resurrection, Sweden, designed by Sigurd Lewerentz.

7.2b

Storefront for Art & Architecture, USA, designed by Steven Holl and Vito Acconci.

7.2c

Groninger Museum, the Netherlands, designed by Philippe Starck.

Object

The deployment of an object can provide focus to a space. Whether the scale of the element is small or large, its use enables movement, supplies rhythm, or balance, and facilitates function.

Object: Study 1

Name: Mandarina Duck Store
Location: Paris, France
Designer: Droog Design

An object, when used at a particular scale, can be the primary organizing element of a space. Instead of just facilitating the arrangement of space, it can control it. Within retail design, the idiosyncratic qualities of an object can communicate an identifiable message that is specifically related to the items for sale. The eccentric or peculiar characteristics of the designed objects can be imbued with the projected lifestyle that the products offer.

Droog created an interior based on a series of elements or cocoons for the flagship Mandarina Duck store in Paris. These objects: circle, tunnel, wall, curtain and enclosure, were then translated into elements for organizing interior space and displaying the collection of bags, clothes and accessories.

7.3a

The enigmatic circular display unit conceals the accessories.

7.3b

Handbags are strapped to the wall element with gigantic rubber bands.

7.3a   7.3b

7.4

The freestanding piece of multi-use furniture stands within a small apartment in New York.

Object: Study 2

Name: Apartment
Location: New York, USA
Designer: George Ranalli

A freestanding object can be designed to accommodate and contain a number of different functions. Separate activities can be collected together to form a tight single element. In a small domestic space, it can be economical to combine the seating, storage, eating, and sleeping activities together, to create one piece of furniture that can contain all of these needs.

In a tiny apartment in a warehouse in New York, George Ranalli has created such a piece of furniture. It consists of a dining space below a raised sleeping platform, which is accessed by a stair that contains bookshelves, with steps that are wide and deep enough to relax upon. The distinct object combines many of the functions necessary to create a suitable space for living.

Object: Study 3

Name: Reactor Film Studio
Location: Los Angeles, USA
Designer: Pugh + Scarpa

A readymade object can create surprise and interest when it is removed from its natural context and placed within unfamiliar surroundings. Despite the fact that conceptual artists have been using found objects for almost a century, it is still a provocative and challenging act for a designer to relocate items that have a specific use and context into a different environment. Pugh + Scarpa installed a shipping container in the "shop window" at the front of the Reactor Film Studio. This unusual element was adapted to contain the meeting room; a small flight of stairs was installed and a door, windows, and other opening were cut into the container. More importantly, it has become a signal of the creative process within the building.

Readymade

Marcel Duchamp developed the term "readymade" in 1915 to refer to found objects chosen by the artist as art. Duchamp assembled the first readymade, "Bicycle Wheel" in 1913, and in 1917, "Fountain," a urinal, which he signed with the pseudonym "R. Mutt," shocked the art world.

7.5a

7.5b

7.5a

The shipping container is remodeled to house the meeting room.

7.5b

The container acts as an advert for the studio in the shop window.

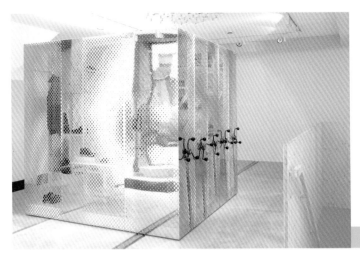

7.6

The library archive units were adapted to display the clothing, shown here in the closed position.

7.6

Object: Study 4

Name: K-Swiss Store
Location: London, UK
Designer: 6a Architects

Familiar objects that are used in an unfamiliar way can provide an interior with a complex and layered ambience. The recognized object has distinct and well-known connotations, and by placing this element within a new or different environment, the designer can exploit the earlier meanings and associations, while also contrasting it with the references to the new space.

This is exactly the approach that 6a Architects took to the design of the K-Swiss store in Hoxton, London. The designers adapted ten library archive units to become storage and display cases in the shop. The library shelves slid on rails to display or enclose the products, and when necessary could glide on the stainless steel rails completely across the space to reveal an open space for music, film, and events. The original sliding shelves spoke of intellectual activity, while the store itself was saturated with a sense of hard physical activity, thus the interior was imbued with the atmosphere exactly suited to the young, trendy, and geeky consumer. Unfortunately, this remarkable little interior has now closed, as fashion always moves quickly if it is to set trends and influence attitudes.

"The partnership between designer and user is a subtle never-ending game. Sometimes the user must be coaxed and taken by the hand—sometimes he can be left safely to take a hint. The designer is in charge and must choose his weapons."

Hugh Casson, *Inscape: the Design of Interiors*. Architectural Press, London 1968

Plane

Whether a wall, floor, or ceiling, a plane will define and organize space.
It controls its visual and physical limits, directs movement, contains texture,
and manipulates light.

Plane: Study 1

Name: Prada Store
Location: New York, USA
Designer: Rem Koolhaas/OMA (Office for Metropolitan Architecture)

A floor can control movement and circulation through a space. The 2001 design of the Prada store in New York manipulated both the physical and visual connection between the front and rear of the shop. The store occupied the ground floor and basement of a very long and narrow nineteenth-century warehouse. The undulating floor exaggerated and amplified the sheer length of the space, to produce what might be described, not as an interior, but as a landscape.

The blonde zebra wood surface swept down from the entrance to unite the basement and ground-floor levels, as a sinuous wave of floor that surfed through the long thin space from ground level into the basement and then back up to realign itself with the entrance at the rear of the shop.

7.7

The undulating horizontal plane links the ground floor with the basement.

7.7

Plane: Study 2

Name: The Brasserie
Location: New York, USA
Designer: Diller Scofidio + Renfro

A plane need not be horizontal, vertical, or flat. The focal point of The Brasserie restaurant, constructed in 2000, is a huge timber surface that wraps around the dining area. It is constructed from a series of interconnected, overlapping sheets of veneered pearwood. The screen is changed and deformed depending upon the function; it is folded to become a bench seat at ground level and it floats vertically to contain the dining area before it is suspended horizontally from the ceiling. Structure and services are concealed behind the screen, thus giving the impression that it is both hovering and unconstrained.

7.8a

7.8a

The pearwood plane wraps around the dining area.

7.8b

7.8b

The plane is constructed from overlapping sheets of veneered pearwood. This allows it to conceal lighting, to become seating, and to define the dining space.

Plane: Study 3

Name: Basilica
Location: Vicenza, Italy
Designer: Andrea Palladio

Palladio's remodeling of the large, slightly uneven town hall (1549) was an ingenious solution to the problem of not only how to support the building, but also how to order and regulate it.

The existing building, which had partially collapsed, was wrapped with a new façade. This solution gives an impression of uniformity to an irregular building and site. Palladio's structure could not be called a building; it was a screen around the existing building that functioned as both a buttressing device and an elegantly decorated wall. The new construction was predetermined by the form of the original building, the position, the height of the two stories, and the width and number of bays.

Classical architecture is ordered and balanced, and Palladio accommodated the existing irregularity by using Serlio's arch-lintel system. The façade was divided into bays, each opening was flanked by columns, and it was the gap between the column and the edge of the bay that absorbed the inconsistencies. Thus, the arches are all the same height and the building appears to be regular.

"The façade is... the most essential architectural element capable of communicating the function and significance of a building... It speaks of the cultural situation at the time that the building was built; it reveals criteria of order and ordering, and gives an account of the possibilities and ingenuity of ornamentation and decoration. A façade also tells us about the inhabitants of a building."

Rob Krier

7.9

7.9

The classical order of the new façade is clearly visible as it wraps around the old building.

Plane: Study 4

Name: Santa Caterina Market
Location: Barcelona, Spain
Designer: EMBT (Enric Miralles–Benedetta Tagliabue)

The Santa Caterina Market reconstruction (2006) was part of a much larger redevelopment of a rundown part of the Gothic Quarter of Barcelona. EMBT have gutted and then recovered the original building with an undulating roof of vivid colors. The architects retained the white painted masonry walls on three sides of the rectangular 1845 market structure, with many arched openings permeable to the surrounding streets. The new roof hovers above these retained walls, scarcely touching or even acknowledging them. It acts as an enormous blanket that controls the climate within the market while still allowing air movement through the building. The undulating structure hangs from four steel arches supported by a steel and timber framework, the exposed services are clearly visible. The roof panels are constructed from laminated timber and the surface is finished in hexagonal ceramic tiles. It is this element that is so vibrant and dramatic, a pixelated representation of the market produce.

7.10a

7.10a

The new roof hovers above the walls of the original building.

7.10b

7.10b

A drawing of the roof in context.

Sequence

The sequence or circulation through a building or space can be vertical or horizontal and usually takes the form of stairs, lifts, corridors, and paths.

Sequence: Study 1

Name: Felix Nussbaum Museum
Location: Osnabrück, Germany
Designer: Daniel Libeskind

The corridor is the backbone of interior circulation, the organization of contemporary space would be impossible without it, and yet strangely, it is a relatively recent invention. It was first used in the seventeenth century as an expedient method of separating the servants from those that they served. The corridor can link spaces and rooms, it can provide a pause, and it can even tell a story.

The architect Daniel Libeskind used this seemingly innocuous element as a narrative device to symbolize the traumatic journey of the persecuted Jewish painter, Felix Nussbaum, in a gallery dedicated to him. The gallery, which is an extension of the old Osnabrück Museum, consists of a series of rooms, each of which is orientated toward one of the various destinations that became a place of refuge for the artist. The galleries contain the paintings that he managed to produce when hidden in the attics or spare rooms of sympathizers, while the interior circulation is a metaphor for this journey. At the end of the final corridor is a symbol of the termination of the painter's flight: a stark metal door with a cross on it.

7.11a

A stark metal door with a cross on it symbolizes the painter's persecution and flight.

7.11b

The emotional journey of Nussbaum's life is evocatively portrayed in the central corridor.

Sequence: Study 2

Name: Great Court, British Museum
Location: London, UK
Designer: Foster + Partners

The staircase provides vertical circulation between floor levels. It can be an uninspiring arrangement, suitable only as an emergency exit, or it can be an elaborate sculptural form that creates a focal point for the interior.

The British Museum, constructed between 1823 and 1859 by Sir Robert Smirke, is one of London's main tourist attractions. The clearing, refurbishment, and covering of the courtyard by Foster + Partners created a generous circulation and meeting area within the heart of the building. The most dominant feature of the remodeling is the new complex glazed roof that covers this inside/outside space. However, the two elliptical staircases that surround the great circular reading room are a much more sensitive interpretation of the old building. They not only provide access to the restaurant and temporary gallery on the first floor, but they also allow the visitor to observe the activities in the courtyard. They appear as strong and distinguished elements and are constructed from the same Spanish limestone as the rest of the building. They provide a thoughtful and respectful addition to the space.

7.12

7.12

The substantial Spanish limestone staircase, situated inside the courtyard.

Sequence: Study 3

Name: Museum of Applied Arts
Location: Frankfurt, Germany
Designer: Richard Meier

The ramp offers a useful alternative to stairs as a method of moving vertically through a building. It encourages all of the building's users to elegantly glide through a space on a gently inclined plane. The primary disadvantage of the ramp is that it requires large swathes of interior space in order to make it accessible, that is, to comply with building regulations, particularly the Disability Discrimination Act (1995).

The Museum of Arts and Crafts in Frankfurt is a series of gleaming white modernist buildings, collected around the 200-year-old Villa Metzler. The ramp is an axial element that traverses and divides the buildings and is slightly out of alignment with the original house, thus accentuating the differences between the old and new. It protrudes slightly from the building and solemnly rises through the new spaces; it is this sense of movement that is used to link the various levels of the building.

7.13a

7.13b

The ramps provide a dignified and leisurely route to the upper galleries.

The sequence of ramps is bathed in natural light.

Sequence: Study 4

Name: *A Matter of Life and Death*
Location: Film
Directors: Emeric Pressburger and Michael Powell

The escalator or moving staircase is one of the most important modern architectural and design developments. It provides easy access for a large number of people to different levels within a building, thus providing links to related floor levels and activities with a minimum of fuss. It is synonymous with shopping centers, airports, train stations, and department stores.

The concept of the moving staircase was used with great effect in Powell and Pressburger's great wartime movie, *A Matter of Life and*

Death (1946). The protagonist, played by David Niven, has, in the fog over the English Channel, somehow managed to evade death. He lives on to inhabit a brightly colored but somewhat disorderly earth. His guardian angel (Marius Goring) tries to lure him upon a moving staircase towards the highly ordered, but black and white Heaven. The staircase is a significant element within the film, symbolizing the epic journey to the afterlife. So central is this escalator to the story, that in the USA the title of the movie was changed to *Stairway to Heaven*.

Disability Discrimination Acts

The Disability Discrimination Acts of 1995 and 2005 are acts of UK law designed to ensure that disabled people are treated fairly and end discrimination against disabled people. This is paralleled in the EU by the European Commission Directive against discrimination, and similarly in the USA where the Americans with Disabilities Act of 1990 (ADA) is a law that was enacted by Congress that prohibits discrimination based upon disability.

7.14

7.14

The staircase is an allegorical element in the seminal film, *A Matter of Life and Death*, symbolizing the great journey to the afterlife.

Light

Whether natural or artificial, light accentuates objects or spaces, suggests movement and circulation, and aids the understanding of the interior.

Light: Study 1

Name: D.E. Shaw Office and Trading Area
Location: New York, USA
Designer: Steven Holl

Natural and artificial light can be combined to create an indefinite or uncertain atmosphere. The entrance area of the D.E. Shaw & Co. offices, on the top floor of a forty-story tower block in New York, is a perfect white double-story cube. Into the walls of this are carved alcoves and niches. There is an ambiguity to these recesses: some lead to further rooms within the office, some are windows, while others are just there for effect, leading nowhere. They are all colored and lit from within, either naturally or artificially, depending upon the position. The illuminated color is reflected in and around the notched spaces, thus projecting the color towards the room and making very apparent that there are spaces beyond the entrance area. The uncertainty about the function of the alcoves creates a mysterious and enigmatic interior.

7.15

7.15

The illuminated niches provide light for the double height reception space.

Light: Study 2

Name: Dulwich Picture Gallery
Location: London, UK
Designer: Sir John Soane

Natural light can be manipulated to create rooms of great emotion and feeling. Light and shade together can be used to generate a narrative or sequence of differing atmospheres or spaces. Dulwich Picture Gallery (1812) is a very fine example of an interior that makes use of controlled light and movement through a series of rooms.

Francis Bourgeois bequeathed his fine collection of paintings as well as sufficient funds to build a gallery for them, to Dulwich College on two conditions; the first was that Sir John Soane was to be the architect and the second was that the gallery should contain his own mausoleum. The plan form of the building suggests an antique catacomb, a progression of quite bright top-lit galleries. At the center, is a dark side chamber that leads to the mausoleum; a serene reverential space that is bathed in amber-colored natural light, from the yellow glass in the rooftop lantern.

7.16a

7.16a

A progression of bright top-lit galleries.

7.16b

The mausoleum is quite dark in comparison to the galleries.

7.16b

Light: Study 3

Name: The Jane Restaurant
Location: Antwerp, Belgium
Designer: Piet Boon® Studio and Studio Job

The twenty-first century has brought a renewed interest in decoration and a return to ornament. Modern industrial processes mean that techniques that a generation ago were time-consuming and costly to produce, can now be easily manufactured cheaply off-site. This fascination with contemporary ornamentation is expressed through many different materials, from interior elements, including wallpaper, fabrics, soft and hard furnishings, and glass, to exterior elements such as the elevation or façade of complete buildings.

Piet Boon and Studio Job (Job Smeets and Nynke Tynagel) developed a series of decorated windows to illuminate a restaurant that is situated within the chapel of a former military hospital. The 500 unique panels were inspired by the chapel's original function combined with among other things: sunflowers, devils, skulls, babies, dice, apple cores, ice cream cones, croissants, penguins, trophies, gas masks, and birthday cakes. Just as the medieval stained glass window would relate a tale, so these windows tell the stories of good and evil, rich and poor, life and death, as well as good food and religion.

7.17a

The windows, which are a modern interpretation of stained glass, tell contemporary tales of food and love, goodness, religion and compassion.

7.17b

The organization of the interior was dictated by the rhythm of the original windows. The glazing is the moment of brightness in what is a really quite austere room.

7.17a

7.17b

Light: Study 4

Name: Chapel of Resurrection, Woodland Cemetery
Location: Stockholm, Sweden
Date: 1925
Designer: Sigurd Lewerentz

The Chapel of Resurrection is a simple, austere building with a detached classical open portico on the north façade and a wide tri-part window on the south. The entrance is at right angles to the axis of the building, and so the procession enters into the shadows of the nave before turning to face the altar. The interior is lit by just the one large off-center, south-facing window, which floods the altar with brilliant light. The journey is one from the daylight of the cemetery, through the darkness of the portico and the shadows of the nave to the radiant brightness of the altar.

7.18

7.18

The south light
dramatically illuminates
the altar.

Threshold

The threshold marks the distinction between spaces and objects. It can indicate the next part of the journey or become a reminder of things already experienced.

Threshold: Study 1

Name: Storefront for Art & Architecture
Location: New York, USA
Designer: Steven Holl and Vito Acconci

The openings in a façade of a building can be described as the threshold between the inside and the outside. The façade of a building is generally solid: masonry, timber, glass, and the openings are usually the doors and windows.

The storefront for Art & Architecture has an adaptable façade, the solidity of the wall is punctured by a collection of cuts and openings. These are a series of orthogonal cutout panels set into a solid screen wall. The panels are set on pivots that allow them to swing open, and depending upon the time, weather, and the current show, they can be arranged in different compositions. This, in effect, eliminates the straightforward barrier between inside and outside, the gallery and the street. This is especially enchanting at night when the interior light explodes from the gallery inviting viewers into this little slice of inside-out New York space.

7.19

7.19

The panels on the façade pivot open in order to diffuse the distinction between inside and out.

Threshold: Study 2

Name: Comme des Garçons Store
Location: New York, USA
Designer: Future Systems

The threshold is generally regarded as the point of transition from one space to another, that is, the point at which a new experience begins.

The Comme des Garçons store is situated in a particularly tough waterside area of New York. The interior of the shop is stark, bright, and white, and contrasts strongly with the nineteenth-century brick façade and the retained old signage and external industrial fire escapes. The entrance marks the transition between the grime, graffiti, and general debris surrounding the shop and the cool clean interior. This change is acknowledged with an asymmetric tubular entrance structure made entirely from aluminum. It is both raw and refined, clean yet unfinished. The slightly swollen floor of the tube transports the shopper over the threshold; the edgy street attitude slips away and is lost in the white space of the interior.

7.20

The contrast between the graffitied exterior and the shiny new entrance tunnel.

7.20

Threshold: Study 3

Name: National Gallery Extension
Location: London, UK
Designer: Venturi, Scott Brown and Associates

A route through a gallery is often more than a chronological journey through the history of art. The works of art themselves can be exhibited or displayed in a manner that accentuates both the work of art and the building. A relationship between the two can be developed.

The Sainsbury Wing, an extension to the National Gallery in London exploits the axis that runs across and links the two buildings. The long route was continued from the courtyard of the original building into the extension, through a sequence of arches or individual thresholds. The perspective has been manipulated by diminishing the dimension of the arches, thus the journey is exaggerated, and the focal point made clearer. At the end of the sequence is a work by Cima da Conegliano, *The Incredulity of Saint Thomas* (about 1502–04) that seems to prolong the development of the arches.

7.21a

7.21b

7.21a

The painting is part of the sequence.

7.21b

The visual journey continues into and through the threshold.

Threshold: Study 4

Name: Summer Hill Apartments
Location: Lake District, England
Designer: Francis Roberts Architects

The architect or designer can use rhythm and balance to enhance what could otherwise be the fairly ordinary experience of moving through the circulation areas of an interior. These are key places within buildings that distribute space, such as a hall, landing, or foyer, but these necessary areas need not be mundane, they can contain as much character and personality as the rest of the building.

This is the approach the Francis Roberts Architects took with the conversion of a Georgian house into five luxury apartments. The central area contained a small colonnade, but lacked natural light and was fully enclosed. A false wall was constructed immediately behind the colonnade, and a reflective glass screen fitted behind a false door, these key moves provide the interior with an illusion of depth, thus furnishing what was once a small and dark space with light and presence.

7.22
***
Artificial light and a reflective screen provide this internal circulation area at Summer Hill with presence and character.

7.22

Texture

The specific choice of materials imparts character upon a space and establishes a direct relationship between the people who occupy the space and the building itself.

Texture: Study 1

Name: Groninger Museum
Location: Groningen, the Netherlands
Designer: Philippe Starck

The Groninger Museum is a collection of distinct buildings designed by different architects to house the four separate collections held by the museum. Alessandro Mendini was responsible for overseeing the whole project and Philippe Starck designed the pavilion for the applied art collection. The building is a huge circular steel drum positioned upon an apparently floating brick plinth, it has no windows, and the interior is completely controlled by artificial light.

The gallery contains a series of tough, highly engineered glass and steel cases that hold beautiful, delicate porcelain teapots, cutlery, and other objects. A diaphanous curtain surrounds these displays; it hangs from the ceiling and curves around the hard edges of each case, creating a tranquil, almost ethereal atmosphere. The visitors becomes a shadow through the translucent screens as they move through the space.

7.23

7.23

The sinuous curtain controls movement through the display space.

Texture: Study 2

Name: Johan Menswear Shop
Location: Graz, Austria
Designer: Claudio Silvestrin

A designer or architect can choose to work with a very limited palette of materials, which will effectively accentuate the qualities and characteristics of each and emphasize the contrast between them. This restrained style of using texture and surfaces is often referred to as minimalism. Identity can be communicated through this restrained and focused approach.

Claudio Silvestrin uses just three materials to organize and decorate the interior of this retail space. This spare and minimal quality is achieved using putty-colored polished plaster for the walls, shelves, ceiling, and cylindrical changing rooms. The floor is of polished concrete and the long central display plinth that slides through the vaulted space is of limed oak.

The design of the space is uncompromising and exact, everything is worked out to a demanding level and the workmanship is exact and precise, even down to the meticulous two-millimeter shadow gap between the floor and the walls.

7.24

The limited palette of materials creates an atmospheric interior.

7.24

Texture: Study 3

Name: Castelvecchio Museum
Location: Verona, Italy
Designer: Carlo Scarpa

Texture is an important element for organizing space and is generally used in one of two ways: "applied" or "found." "Applied" is the method of cladding or lining a space with a specific material, whereas "found" makes use of existing textures, which are retained and incorporated into the new design.

A common feature of Carlo Scarpa's work was to leave a small gap between new and existing materials, thus creating clarity and emphasizing both, and an example of this can be seen at the Castelvecchio Museum (1964). The new stone floors of the galleries stop short of the existing walls. The vertical pink Prun stone slabs, which are placed at the threshold of each room and accentuate the junction between new and old, are slightly proud, and the sculptures are separated from the floor and placed upon floating plinths.

"A coarse rough concrete finish has a quite different quality to that of polished marble and different again to studded rubber or fun fur, even though they can all quite viably be placed in an identical position."

Brooker & Stone

7.25

7.25

The polished pigmented plaster of the display screen highlights the delicate qualities of the objects.

Texture: Study 4

Name: Churchgate House
Location: Manchester, UK
Designer: Atelier MB

The designer can use a particular material or texture to tie a long, irregular, or disconnected interior together. A single distinctive and specific detail can create a link between disparate spaces; it can aid navigation through what could be anonymous areas and create a unifying identity. This is the tactic that Atelier MB has taken to the remodeling of the foyer area of Churchgate House. The building was expanded to accommodate a large collection of different users, and so the foyer is required to act as a collective hub for all of these. The designers achieved this with a characteristic yet limited palette of materials, the most distinctive elements within this are the backlit limed oak faceted screens and the Manchester brick-red heavy woven woolen upholstery. This has created an interior that reflects the strategic importance of its position within the building, while also fusing together a collection of individual spaces.

7.26

The simple modulated limed oak screen ties different areas of the interior together. The wall immediately behind the reception desk is illuminated, while the partition at the edge of the foyer space is flat.

7.26

Glossary

Adaptation
The process of transforming an existing building to accommodate new uses. This is also referred to as remodeling, adaptive reuse, and interior architecture.

Analysis
The act of exploring and studying an existing building. This can be done in a variety of ways in order to extract the meaningful qualities of the building to prompt or stimulate the process of transforming the space.

Applied texture
Added material such as metal, fabric, plastic, or timber that can be applied to an existing surface in order to create or shape the new visual and atmospheric identity of an interior.

Arch
A structural device that allows openings to be formed in a wall or façade. It is a curved structure, capable of spanning a space while supporting the significant weight of the wall above.

Axis
An imaginary line that usually runs through the center of a space or building, it is used as a planning device and is related to symmetry. Axial planning can be used to arrange an interior in straight lines or in a way that prioritizes certain qualities such as a view through the space or emphasizes hierarchy.

Baroque
The style of the seventeenth century that fostered an exuberant period in all of the arts. In architecture, the Baroque style was characterized by a florid, theatrical style, distinguished by elaborating Renaissance style elements in a sculptural and exaggerated fashion.

Beam
A core component of a basic structural frame. It is a horizontal bar, usually made from masonry, steel, or timber that is supported at either end.

Circulation
The methods of movement within a building. It is often arranged as a series of horizontal routes through a building via walkways, corridors and bridges, or vertically via stairs, ramps, lifts, and escalators.

Cladding
The application of a layer of material that will cover the structure of a building or element. On the outside of a building, this may have to consider weathering and climate control. In an interior, cladding is more important in terms of performance, look, and identity. The relationship between cladding and structure and its visual appearance is a complex issue that dominates architectural and design history. See Loos's *Ornament and Crime*, 1908.

Classical
Classical architecture derives its principles from Greek and Roman art and architecture. The main orders of classical architecture are Tuscan, Doric, Ionic, Corinthian, and Composite. In its revived style known as neoclassicism.

Column
The column, along with the beam, forms the basic component of the structural system. It is the vertical element of the frame and is usually made from masonry, steel, or timber.

Composition
The plan or arrangement of elements in a visual design. In interior planning, it relates to the organization of the components of space. In elevations or sections, composition can relate to the deployment of rooms and interior elements in the building.

Conservation
The art of conserving existing structures in their present form or returning them back to their original state.

Context
The conditions surrounding the building to be reused. These conditions may be in close proximity or far away and have a variety of impacts upon the new interior.

Design process
The method by which a new design is created and realized.

Detail
The finalizing of a space and the application of materials and surfaces to an interior scheme is known as detailing. This often involves joinery, the application of materials and sometimes prototyping through mock-ups and samples.

Element
Within an interior, a specific object such as a piece of furniture or a room is described as an "element" within the space.

Elevation
An elevation is a drawing usually of an outside wall or façade of a building. It is a two-dimensional representation of a wall showing the position of windows, doors, and any other details of the building exterior.

Environment
Environment refers to the context of a building and its interior, and also refers to climatic issues with the design scheme or existing building.

Façade
Quite simply the exterior front plane of a building.

Form follows form
The notion that the design of an interior space is influenced by the qualities of the space in which it is being built.

Form follows function
"Form follows function" is the modernist declaration that new buildings and interior spaces are determined by the functions that take place inside of them.

Found texture
When working with existing buildings, surfaces within the space can be retained and used to provide meaningful connections to the original site.

Fractal
A geometric shape that can be subdivided into parts, all of which are a reduced-size copy of the whole. Fractal relates to unusual geometries that may be used to generate complex and unusual forms for building design; this may need the help of sophisticated computer software.

Free plan
A system of design that uses a framed structure, and thus removes the need for load-bearing walls, creating a freedom and flexibility to the space.

Function
The use of a space, either new or old, will often be referred to as the function of the space. Quite often function will also be referred to as "the program" of the interior or the accommodation brief for the new design.

Geometry
Geometry is the field of studying the spatial relationships between things and is closely related to mathematics. In architecture and design, it relates to the systematic organization of building spaces and elements.

Gothic Revival
The Gothic Revival was an architectural movement that originated in England in the nineteenth century and sought to revive the medieval or pointed style in response to the prevailing neoclassical style of the time.

Hierarchy
When organizing and planning space, the word hierarchy is sometimes used to distinguish primary and secondary elements within a design. It may also be used to classify major and minor functions within a space.

HVAC
Acronym for heating, ventilation, and air conditioning.

Interior architecture
Interior architecture is the practice of remodeling existing buildings. As well as the robust reworking of a building, interior architecture often deals with complex structural, environmental, and servicing problems. It is sometimes referred to as adaptation, adaptive reuse, or remodeling.

Interior decoration
Interior decoration is the art of decorating inside spaces and rooms to impart a particular character and atmosphere to the room. It is often concerned with such issues as surface pattern, ornament, furniture, soft furnishings, and lighting.

Interior design

Interior design is an interdisciplinary practice that is concerned with the creation of a range of interior environments that articulate identity and atmosphere, through the manipulation of spatial volume, the placement of specific objects and furniture, and the treatment of surfaces.

Listed building

When a building, interior, monument, or bridge is considered to be of historic importance or of cultural significance and therefore in need of protection from demolition or any insensitive changes, it is placed upon a protected building list. The listing usually takes the form of a grading of importance from one through to three.

Load bearing

Load bearing is a term that refers to the structural system employed to construct the building. It refers to a structure that is usually masonry and built up brick by brick from the ground.

Monocoque

A construction technique that uses the external skin of the object for structural support. The internal structure and the skin are unified as a single element. This is a method of construction most prevalent in aircraft and automotive design, but is beginning to be used as an architectural construction technique.

Narrative

Narrative is a story or a text that describes a sequence of characters and events. In architecture and design, narrative is used to describe the stories or the sequence of events that the designer may wish to convey: whether an existing building, an exhibition design, or the concept or brand identity of a space.

Object

A purposefully placed object is loaded with meaning; whether it is a small piece of furniture, a large sculpture, or a number of pieces clustered together, it establishes a physical and cultural relationship with its environment.

Organization

Organization can be described as the planning or arrangement of a space; that is the objects, rooms, and elements.

Ornament

An ornament is a decorative detail than can be used to embellish parts of a building or an interior. It is often superfluous, and it became a highly debated element of design in the twentieth century.

Plan libre

See *Free plan*.

Plane

The façade, wall, ceiling, and floor are regarded as the essential planes of the interior and a building.

Planning

The organization of an interior by arranging the rooms, spaces and structure in a two-dimensional drawing.

Playstation organization

An organizational technique where a collection of events or objects are arranged in series, each is a complete entity and has to be fully appreciated before the viewer or competitor can move on. Similar to the organizational technique used in computer games.

Portico

A roofed space, often open or partly enclosed that forms the entrance to a building It developed in early Greek architecture, and is often supported by columns and can be a grand device on the façade of a building.

Promenade

One of Le Corbusier's "Five Points of Architecture", it is the modernist concept of continual movement through a building. This journey is also referred to as architectural promenade.

Raumplan

The Viennese architect Adolf Loos devised the *Raumplan* (space plan), it is best exemplified in the designs for the Müller and Moller houses in Prague and Vienna. The houses consist of a series of compact, enclosed, and intimately connected rooms. Movement between them often organized in a complex manner.

Readymade

The development of art from utilitarian everyday found objects not normally considered as art in their own right. The term "readymade" was coined by the artist, Marcel Duchamp, who created a series of objet d'art from such off-the-peg items as a bicycle wheel, a bottle rack, and a urinal.

Remodeling

The process of wholeheartedly altering a building. The function is the most obvious change, but other alterations may be made to the building such as its structure, circulation routes, and its orientation. Additions may be constructed while other areas may be demolished.

Renovation

Renovation is the process of renewing and updating a building. The function will remain the same and the structure is generally untouched, but the manner in which the building is used will be brought up to date. It is usually the services that require attention, especially the heating and sanitary systems.

Restoration

The process of returning the condition of the building to its original state, often involving materials and techniques of the original period.

Reuse

The transformation of an existing building, reuse suggests that the elements and parts of both new and old buildings are reworked in order to create a new space. See also *Adaptation*, *Remodeling*, and *Interior architecture*.

Section

At any point on the plan of a building, the designer may describe a line through the drawing and visualize a vertical cut through the spaces. This is called a section, it will explain the volumes of the spaces and indicate the position of the walls, the floors, the roof, and other structural elements.

Sequence

The order of interior spaces that the designer intends the visitor to experience in their journey through the space.

Site-specific

The site is the specific location or context of a building or space. Site-specific is a phrase used to describe the influences that are derived directly from the particular conditions found on site.

Spolia

Spolia describes the act of reusing building elements and applying them to new or later monuments. It derives from the phrase "the spoils of war" where the victors in battle would take trophies from their foes.

Structure

A shelter or an enclosure that distinguishes inside and outside space. Structure is one of the basic elements of the construction of space and usually takes the form of materials assembled in such a way as to withstand the pressures put upon them.

Sustainability

In architecture and design, the sensible use of natural resources in the construction and design industry, materials used in a way that does not deplete them in an unnecessary or wasteful way. Sustainability also refers to the sourcing and use of methods of construction and certain materials that do not contribute to climate change through the exhaustion of natural resources or their transport across the world.

Threshold

The threshold is the point of transition between two spaces, whether this is inside and outside, or two interior spaces.

Truss

A truss is a number of beams and/or rafters tied together to form a bridging element.

Weatherboarding

A cladding method that uses timber to cover a building by successively overlapping each member, thus allowing the rain to run off and make a watertight seal.

Further Reading

Alexander, C. 1977. *A Pattern Language*. Oxford: Oxford University Press

Andrea Palladio quoted in Marton, P., Pape, T., Wundram, M. 2004. *Palladio: The Complete Buildings*. Köln: Taschen

Blazwick, I. and Wilson, S. 2000. *Tate Modern: The Handbook*. London: Tate Publishing

Blunder Jones, P. and Canniffe, C. 2007. *Modern Architecture Through Case Studies 1945–1990*. London: Architectural Press

Brooker, G. and Stone, S. 2004. *Re-Readings: Interior architecture and the design principles of remodeling existing buildings*. London: RIBA Publishing

Brooker, G. and Stone, S. 2008. *Basics Interior Architecture: Context and Environment*. AVA

Brooker, G. and Stone, S. 2009. *Basics Interior Architecture: Elements and Objects*. AVA

Brooker, G. and Stone, S. 2013. *From Organisation to Decoration: A Routledge Reader of Interiors*. London: Routledge

Buchanan, P., Kogod, K., Montaner, J.M. 1990. *The Architecture of Enric Miralles and Carme Pinōs*. Santa Fe: Lumen Books

Burkhardt, F. 1997. *Domus Dossier*. Issue 5

Codman, O. and Wharton, E. 1898. *The Decoration of Houses*. London: B.T. Batsford

Cohen, M. 2002. p.53. *Domus 853*

Cook, P. 1995. *Primer*. London: Academy Editions

Cramer, J. and Breitling, S. 2007. *Architecture in Existing Fabric: Planning, Design and Building*. Birkhauser

Cullen, G. 1996. *The Concise Townscape*. Oxford: The Architectural Press

Diller, E. and Scofidio, R. 1994. *Flesh: Architectural Probes*. London: Triangle Architectural Publishing

Energy Research Group (Owen Lewis, J. (ed)). 1999. *A Green Vitruvius: Principles and Practice of Sustainable Architectural Design*. London: James & James (Science Publishers)

Fiell, C. and Fiell, P. 1997. *1000 Chairs*. Köln: Taschen

Frampton, K. 1980. *Modern Architecture: A Critical History*. London: Thames & Hudson

Gregotti, V. 1996. *Inside Architecture*. Cambridge, MA: MIT Press

Hebly, A. in Risselada, M. (ed.). 1989. *Raumplan Versus Plan Libre*. New York: Rizzoli

Holl, S. 1989. *Anchoring: Selected Projects 1975–1988*. New Jersey: Princeton Architectural Press

Johan Jessen and Jochem Schneider, quoted in Schittich, C. (ed). 2003. *Building in Existing Fabric*. Berlin: Birkhäuser Edition Detail

Koolhaas, R. 1998. *OMA/Rem Koolhaas 1987–1998*. Madrid: El Croquis

Krier, R. 1988. *Architectural Composition*. London: Academy Editions

Krier, R. 1983. *Elements of Architecture*. London: Architectural Design, Profile 49

Lazzarini, C. 1998. *Frame Magazine*. July/August 1998

Le Corbusier, É. J. 1923. *Towards a New Architecture*. Paris

Littlefield, D. and Lewis, S. 2007. *Architectural Voices*. Chichester: Wiley

Lootsma, B. 2000. *SuperDutch: New Architecture in the Netherlands*. New Jersey: Princeton Architectural Press

Massey, A. 1990. *Interior Design of the 20th Century*. London: Thames & Hudson

Massey, A. 2008. *Interior Design since 1900*, 2nd Ed. London: Thames and Hudson

Montaner, J.M. 1990. Basic Formal Concepts in Miralles' and Pinōs' Work. In: Buchanan, P., Moore, R. 1992. *Sackler Galleries, Royal Academy*. London: Blueprint Extra 04

Pallasmaa, J. 2005. *Encounters. Architectural Essays*. Helsinki: Rakennustieto

Penoyre, G. and Prasad, S. 2014. *Retrofit for Purpose: Low Energy Renewal of Non-Domestic Buildings*. London: RIBA Publishing

Pile, J. 2013. *A History of Interior Design*, 4th Ed. London: Laurence King

Porter, T. 1997. *The Architect's Eye*. London: E&FN Spon

Praz, M. 1982. *An Illustrated History of Interior Decoration*. London: Thames and Hudson

Preston, J. and Taylor, M. 2006. *Intimus: Interior Design Theory Reader*. Chichester: Wiley

Ranalli, G. 1984. The Coherence of a Quest. In: Dal Co, F. Mazzariol, G. 1984. *Carlo Scarpa: The Complete Works*. Milan: Electa Editrice/Rizzoli

Robert, P. 1989. *Adaptations: New uses for old buildings*. New Jersey: Princeton Architectural Press

Rowe, C. and Koetter, F. 1984. *Collage City*. MIT

Schittich, C. ed. 2003. *In Detail: Building in Existing Fabric: Refurbishment, Extensions, New Designs*. Birkhauser: Publishers for Architecture

Schumacher, T. 1996. Contextualism: Urban Ideals and Deformations. In: Nesbitt, K. (ed). *Theorizing a New Agenda for Architecture Theory*. New Jersey: Princeton Architectural Press

Scott, F. 2007. *On Altering Architecture*. Routledge

Sparke, P. 2008. *The Modern Interior*. London: Reaktion Books

Strike, J. 1994. *Architecture In Conservation*. Routledge

Thornton, P. 1993. *Authentic Décor: The Domestic Interior 1620–1920*. London: Weidenfeld and Nicolson

Turrell, J. 1987. *Mapping Spaces: A topological survey of the work of James Turrell*. New York: Peter Blum Editions

Van Doesburg, T. 1924. "Tot een beeldende architectuur." *De Stijl*. 1 (6/7) p.80 In: Padovan, R. 2002. *Towards Universality: Le Corbusier, Mies and De Stijl.* London: Routledge

Vesely, D. 2004. *Architecture in the Age of Divided Representation*. Cambridge, MA: MIT Press

Weston, R. 2002. *Modernism*. London: Phaidon

Index

Acknowledgments and Image Credits

Graeme and Sally would like to thank Kate Duffy and Leafy Cummins for their patience and support and help during the construction of the book. Graeme would like to thank Claire for being such a stalwart, and Sally gratefully acknowledges the forbearance of Dominic, Reuben, Ivan and Agnes exhibited during the indulgence of writing.

Cover Nils Petter Dale and Ivan Brodey; p3 0.1 Paul Warchol; p7 0.2 Christian Richters; p14–15 1.5a, 1.5b, 1.5c, 1.5d Ben Kelly Design; p22 1.9a Chicago History Museum/Getty; p26 2.1 Howard Powsney; p33 2.4a, 2.4b OMI Architects; p33 2.4c, 2.4d Jonathan Keenan; p37 2.6c O.M. Ungers; p40 2.8a Brian Yates/Malcolm Fraser; p48 2.12a JVA; p49 2.12b Nils Petter Dale and Ivan Brodey; p55 2.15a, 2.15b, 2.15c, 2.15d, 2.15e Rolant Dafis; p57 2.16a, 2.16b, 2.16c Photographs by Jack Hobhouse; p62–63 2.19a, 2.19b Misae Hiromatsu (Beijing Ruijing Photo); p64 3.1 SOL89; p69 3.2a, 3.2b, 3.2c –Clegg Bradley Studios; p70–71 3.3a, 3.3b Malcolm Fraser Architects; p72–73 3.4a, 3.4b, 3.4c SOL89; p74 4.1 Photograph by Jack Hobhouse; p81 4.4a, 4.4b, 4.4c Kengo Kuma Associates; p96–97 4.12a, 4.12b, 4.12c, 4.12d 3Gatti; p99 4.13d, 4.13e, 4.13f, 4.13g MVRDV; p102 5.1 Francis Roberts Architects; p108 5.4a, 5.4b, 5.4c John Linden; p111 5.5a, 5.5b Jonathan Keenan; p111 5.5c OMI Architects; p116 5.8a, 5.8b HGA; p116 5.8c, 5.8d, 5.8e Reio Avaste; p119 5.9a, 5.9c, 5.9d Andrew Wuttke Photography; p119 5.9b Breathe Architecture; p120–121 5.10a, 5.10b © Chris Gascoigne/View; p122–123 5.11a, 5.11b, propeller z; p123 5.11c, 5.11d Margherita Spiluttini/ propeller z; p128–129 6.3a 6.3b, 6.3c 6A Architects; p129 6.3d, 6.3e David Grandorge/6A Architects; p132–133 6.5a, 6.5b, 6.5c Duilio Forte; p136 6.7a Lazzarini Pickering Studio; p137 6.7b, 6.7c Photos Matteo Piazza; p139 6.8b, 6.8c, 6.8d Diller Scofidio + Renfro; p142 6.10a SOMA; p143 6.10b, 6.10c, 6.10d David Lee, Palm Springs, CA; p144 6.11a Ronan and Erwan Bouroullec; 145 6.11b, 6.11c, 6.11d, 6.11e © Morgane Le Gall; p146 7.1 design: Studio Job / material: polychrome ceramic pigments sintered into the surface of glass panels / dimensions: 105 m2 divided over 15 windows / compositions: over 500 unique glass panels / production: Steinfort Glass BV / restaurant: Sergio Herman and Nick Bril / interior: Piet Boon, Amsterdam / photography Loek Blonk, Eric Kleinberg / The Jane Paradeplein, 2018 Antwerp, Belgium http://thejaneantwerp.com/; p150 7.3a, 7.3b Winter Vandenbrink; p151 7.4 George Cserna; p152 7.5a, 7.5b Marvin Rand; p157 7.10b EMBT; p158 7.11a © Peter Mackinven/ View; p161 7.14 Rex Features; p162 7.15 Paul Warchol; p164 7.17a 7.17b design: Studio Job / material: polychrome ceramic pigments sintered into the surface of glass panels / dimensions: 105 m2 divided over 15 windows / compositions: over 500 unique glass panels / production: Steinfort Glass BV / restaurant: Sergio Herman and Nick Bril / interior: Piet Boon, Amsterdam / photography Loek Blonk, Eric Kleinberg / The Jane Paradeplein, 2018 Antwerp, Belgium http:// thejaneantwerp.com/; p173 7.26 Howard Powsney.

Pictures not credited belong to the authors.